MUSHROOM COLORING BOOK

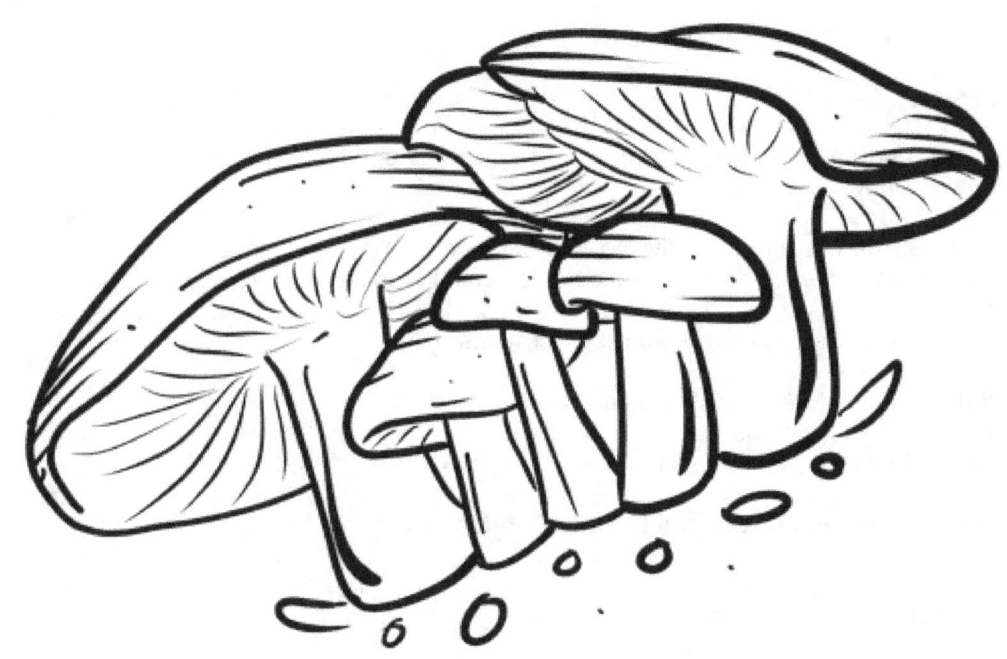

Dr. Melissa Caudle

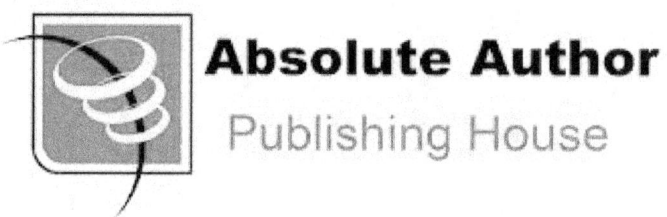

MUSHROOM COLORING BOOK

Copyright ©2022 by Dr. Melissa Caudle

ALL RIGHTS RESERVED

No drawing can be copied, printed, or reproduced in any form without the written consent of Dr. Melissa Caudle.

Coloring Hints: It is strongly advised that each colorist place a piece of cardstock or file folder behind each page as you color to avoid bleed through. This is especially important when using markers or watercolor. For two-side coloring books, I recommend only using colored pencils or crayons.

Publisher: Absolute Author Publishing House
Editor: Dr. Carol Michaels
Cover Designer: Dr. Melissa Caudle

Library of Congress Catalogue In-Data Publication

p. cm.

Hardback ISBN: 978-1-64953-674-7
Paperback ISBN: 978-1-64953-675-4

About the Author

Dr. Melissa Caudle is an award-winning screenwriter, illustrator, and bestselling author with over 100 books for adults and children.

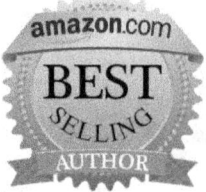

PRINTED IN THE UNITED STATES OF AMERICA

COLOR TEST PAGES

COLOR TEST PAGES

COLOR TEST PAGES

COLOR TEST PAGES

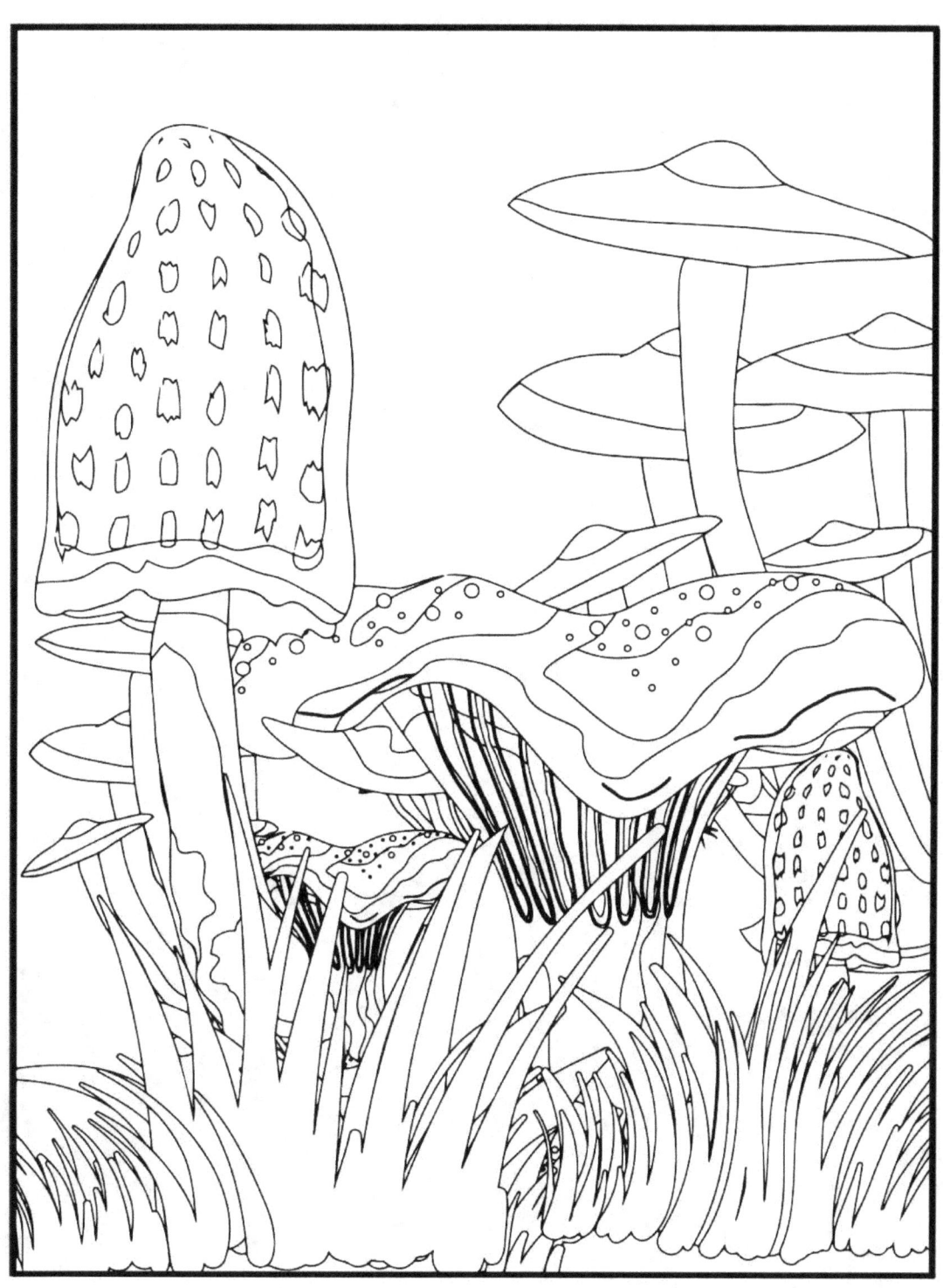

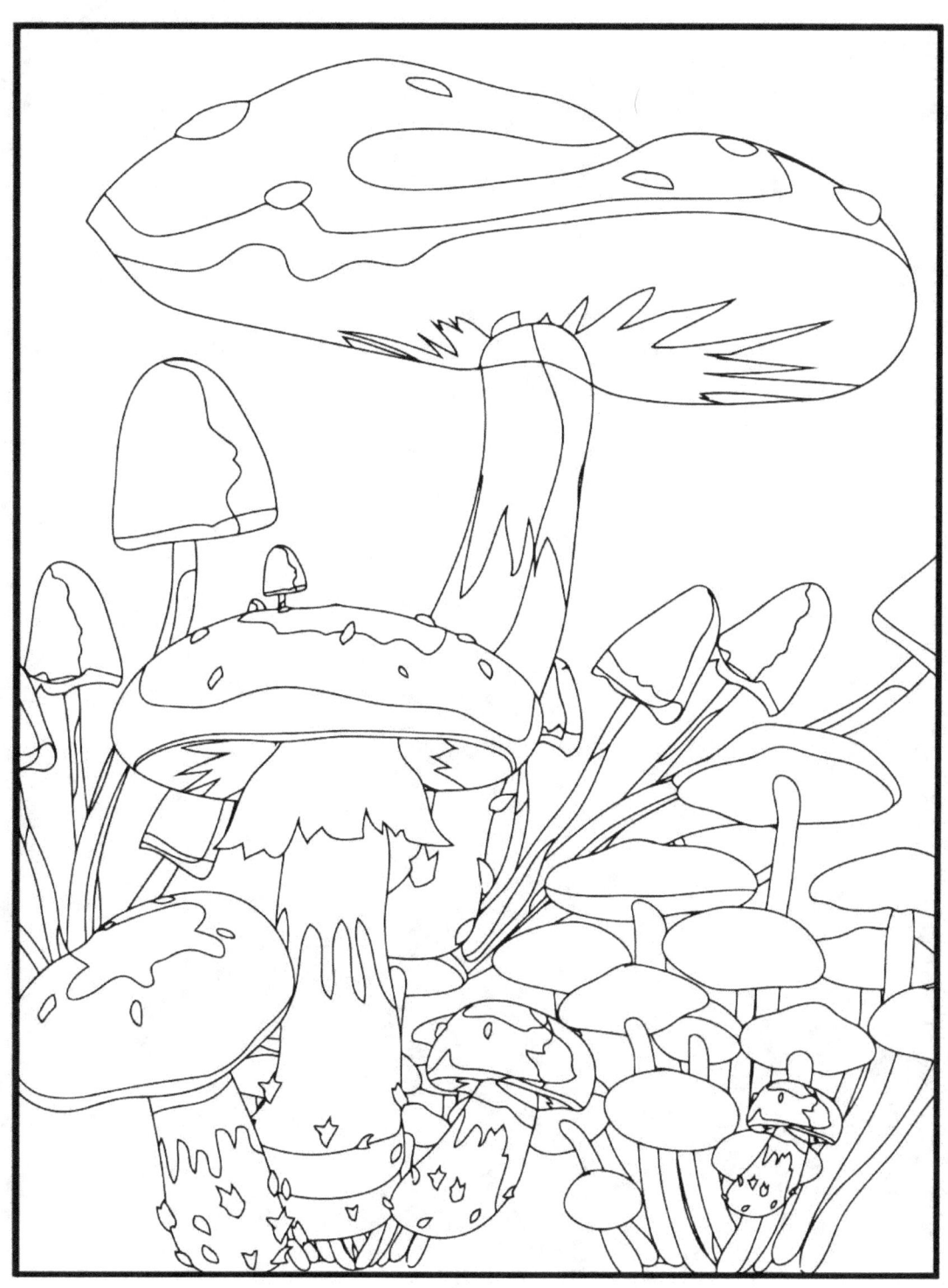

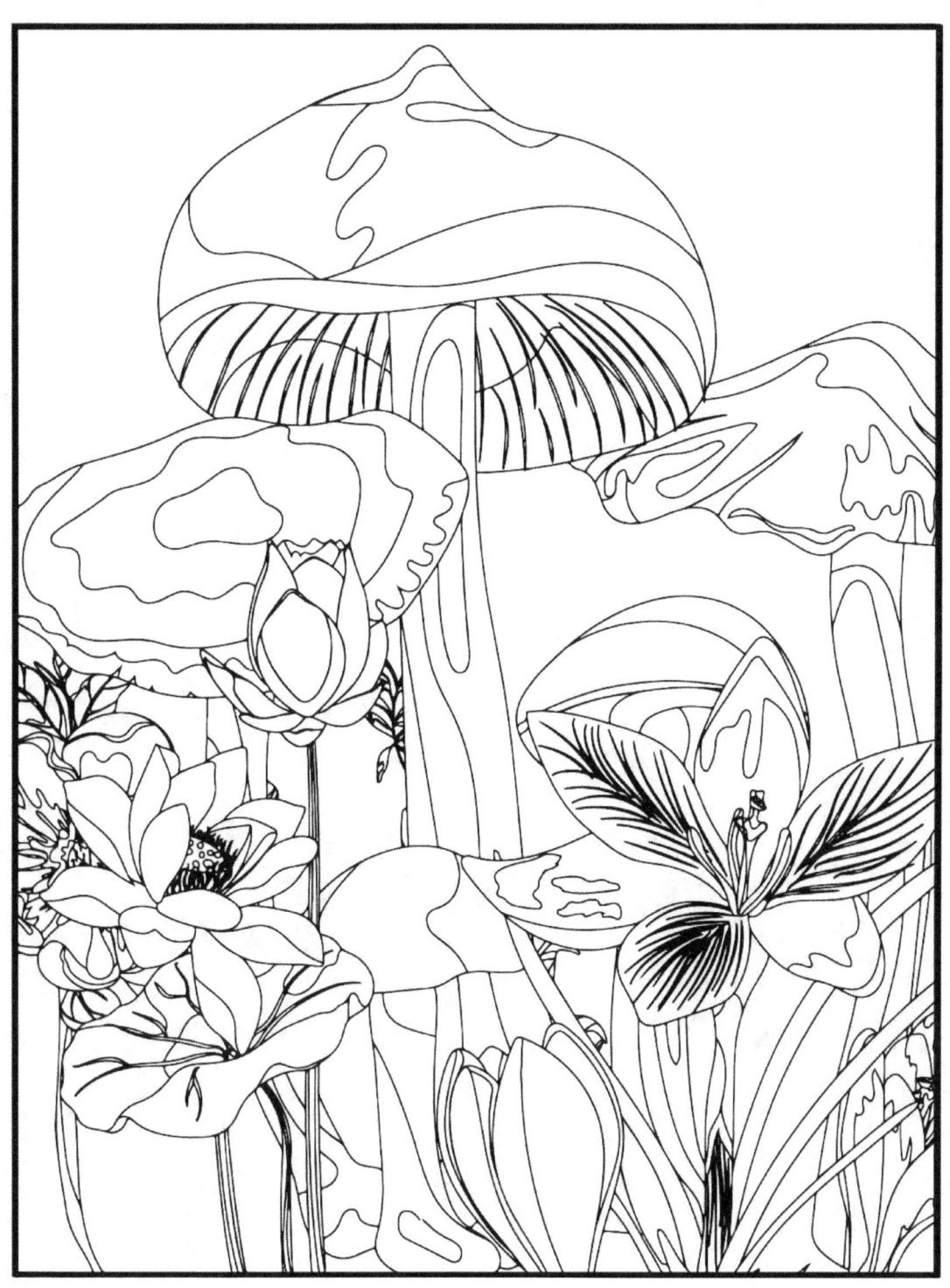

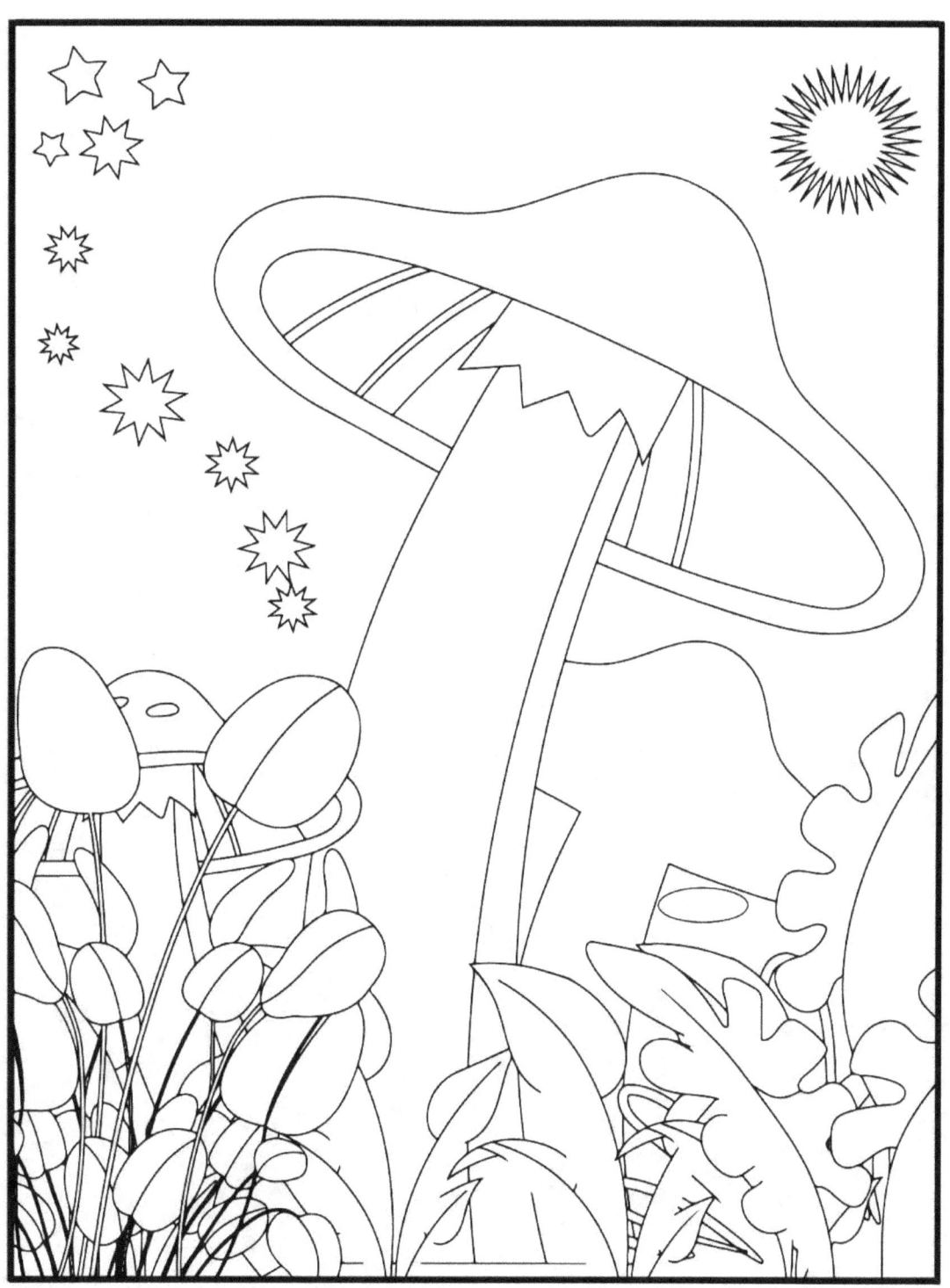

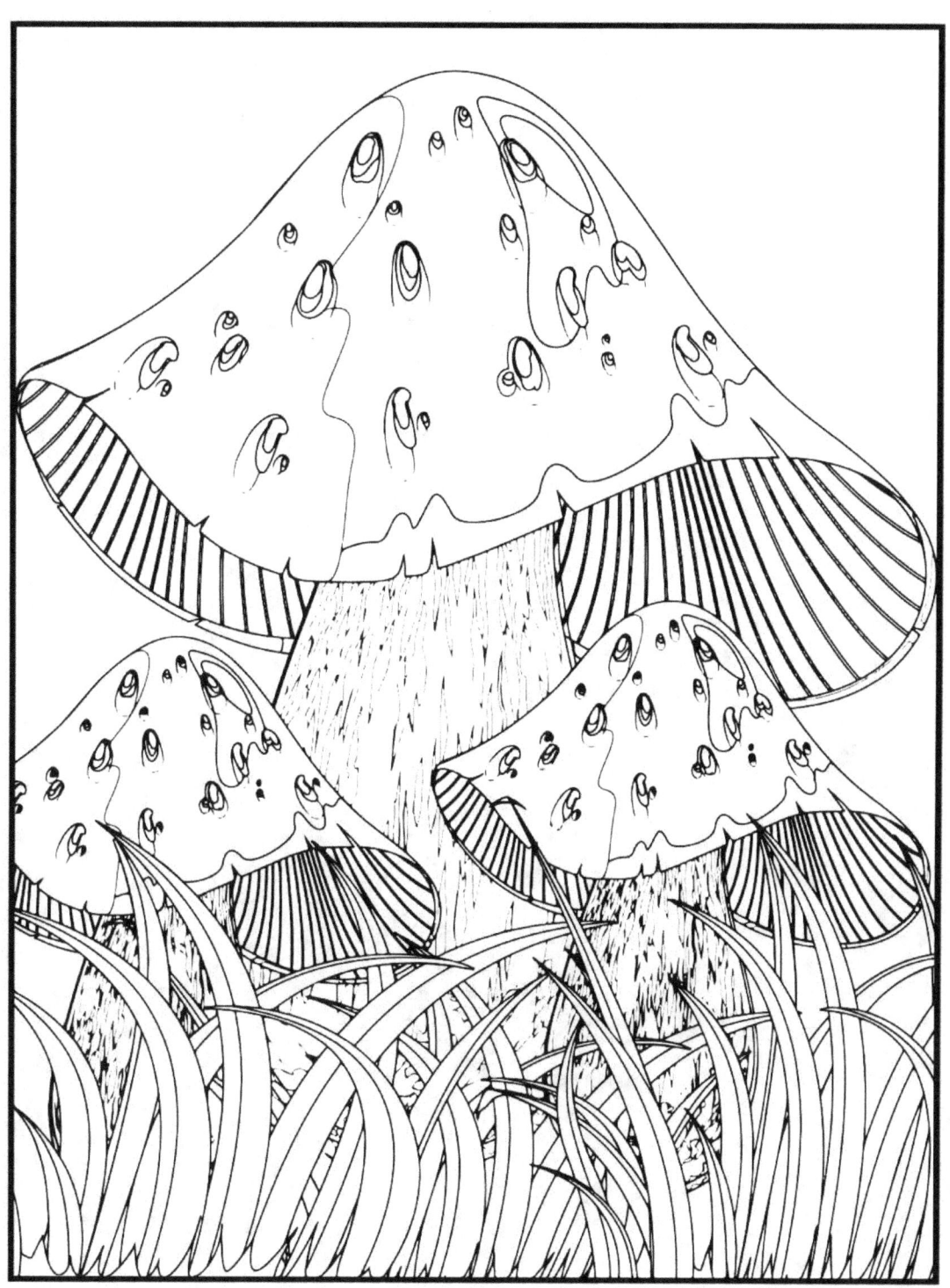

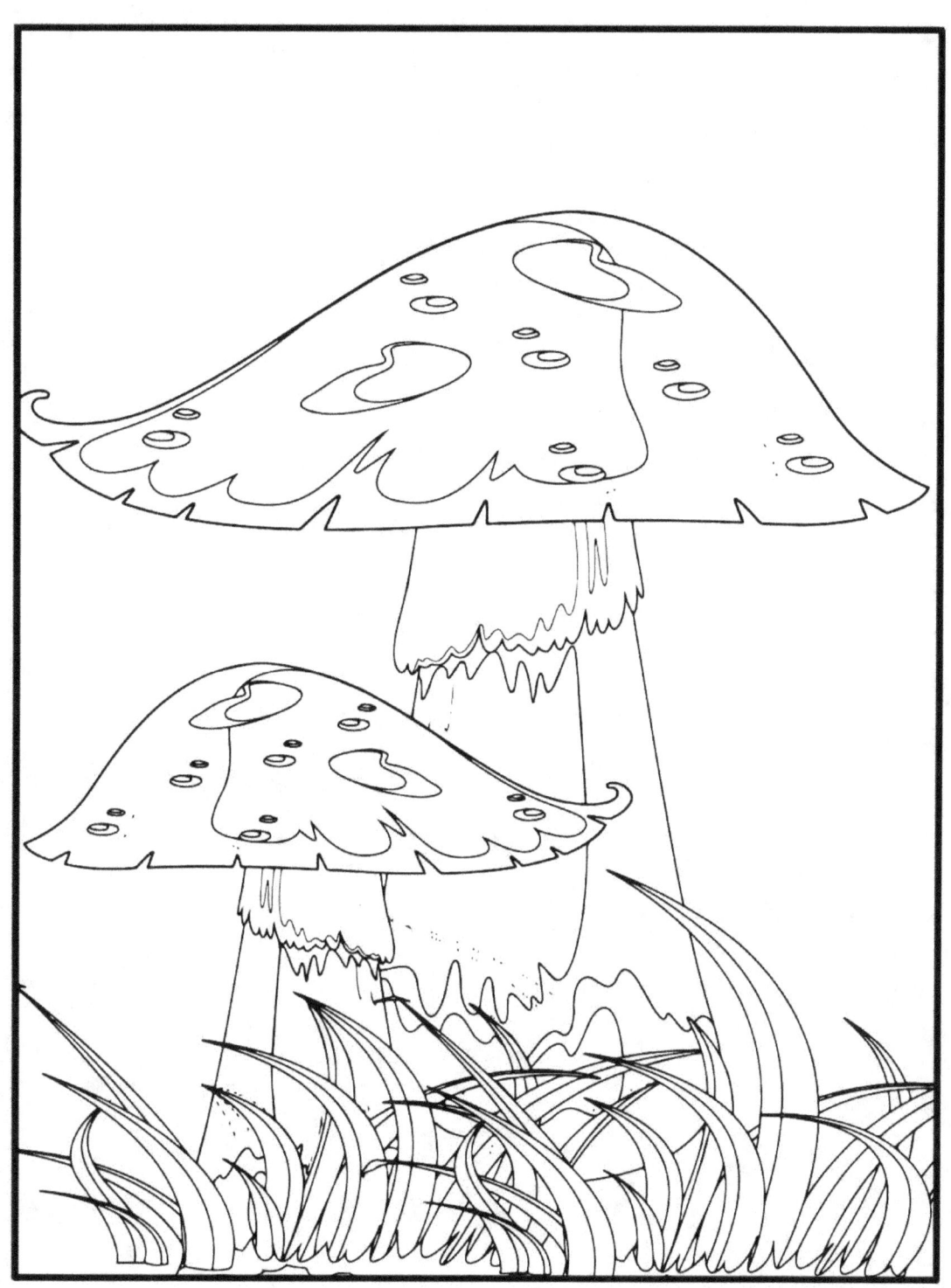

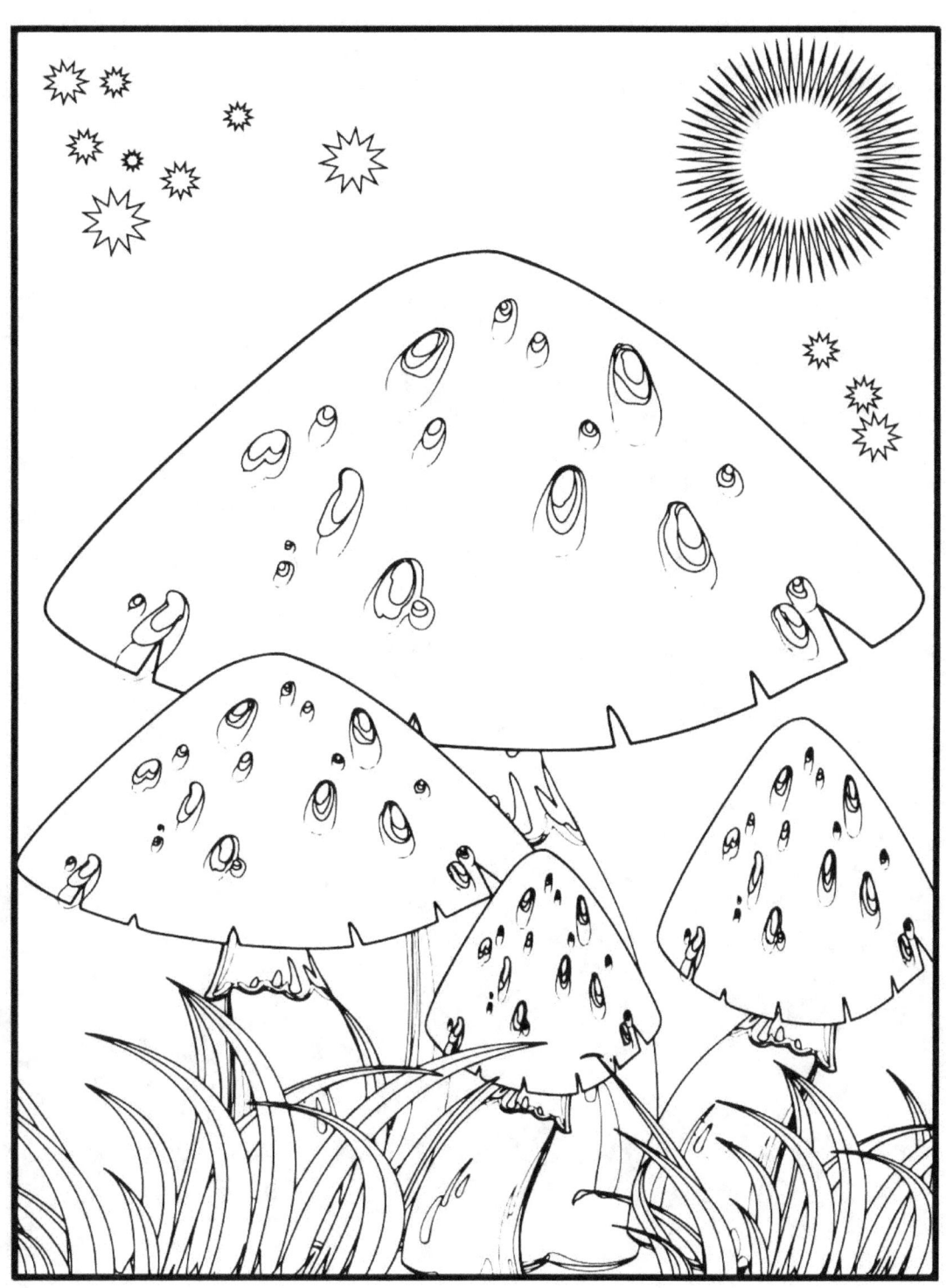

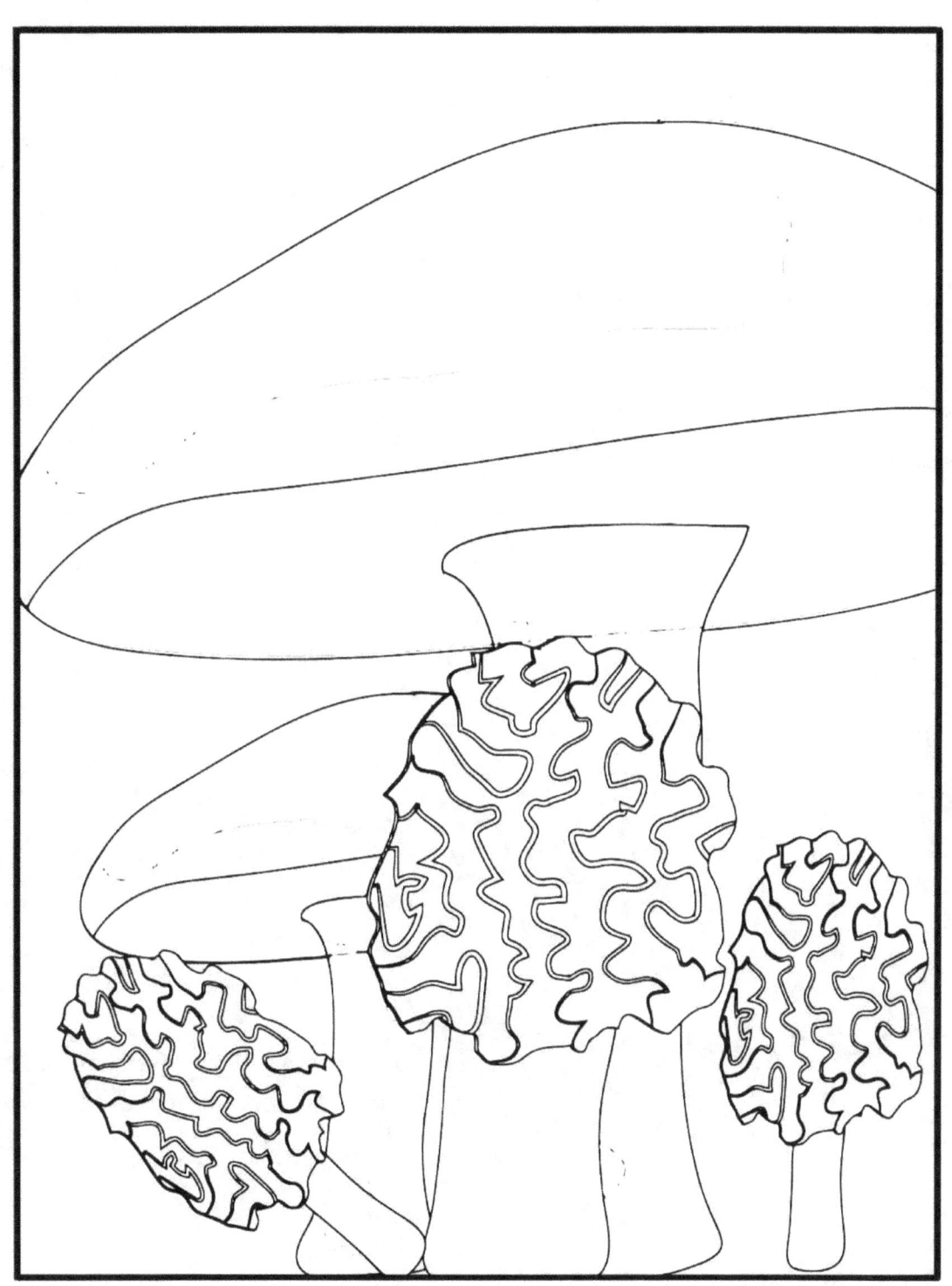

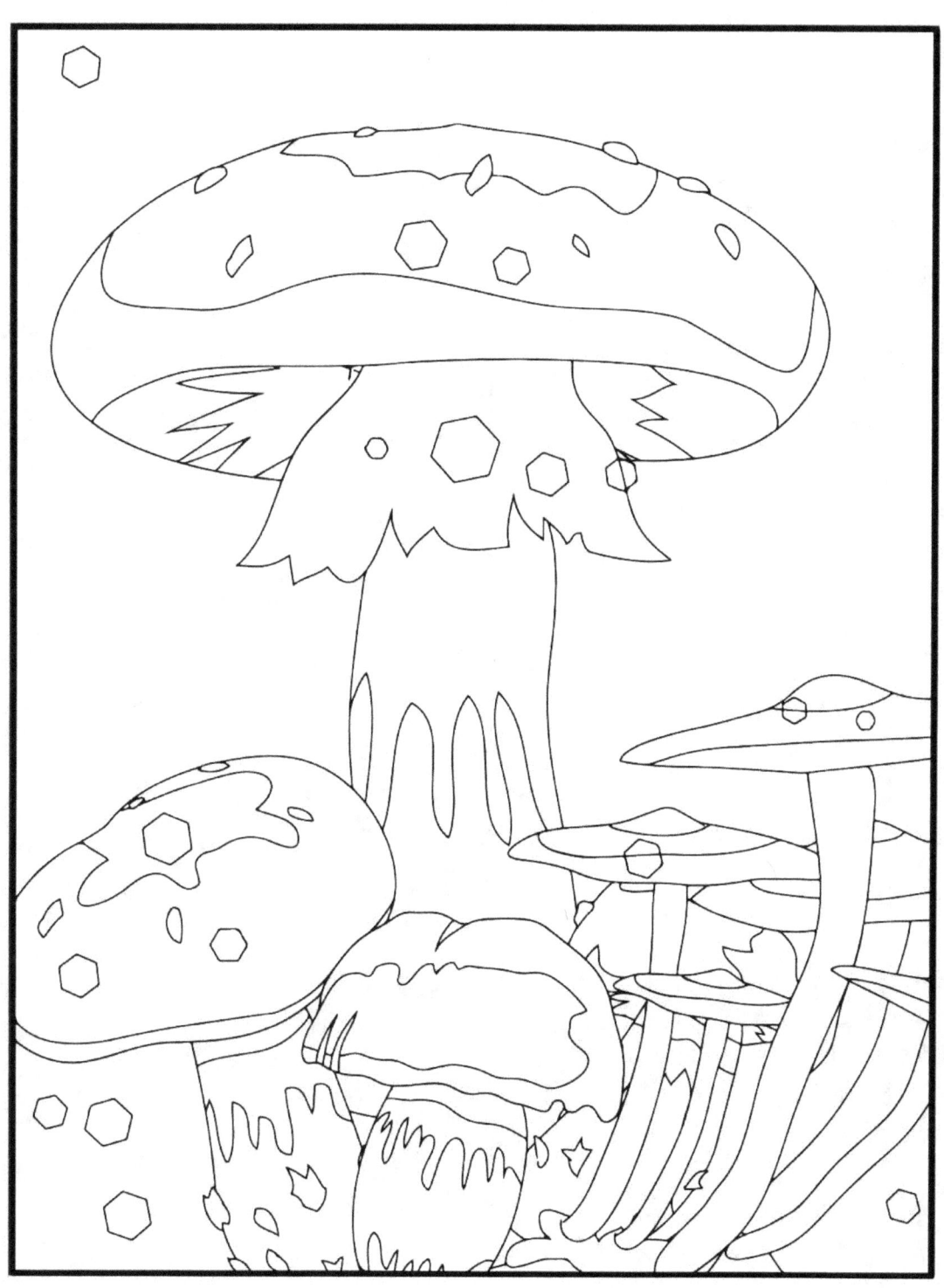

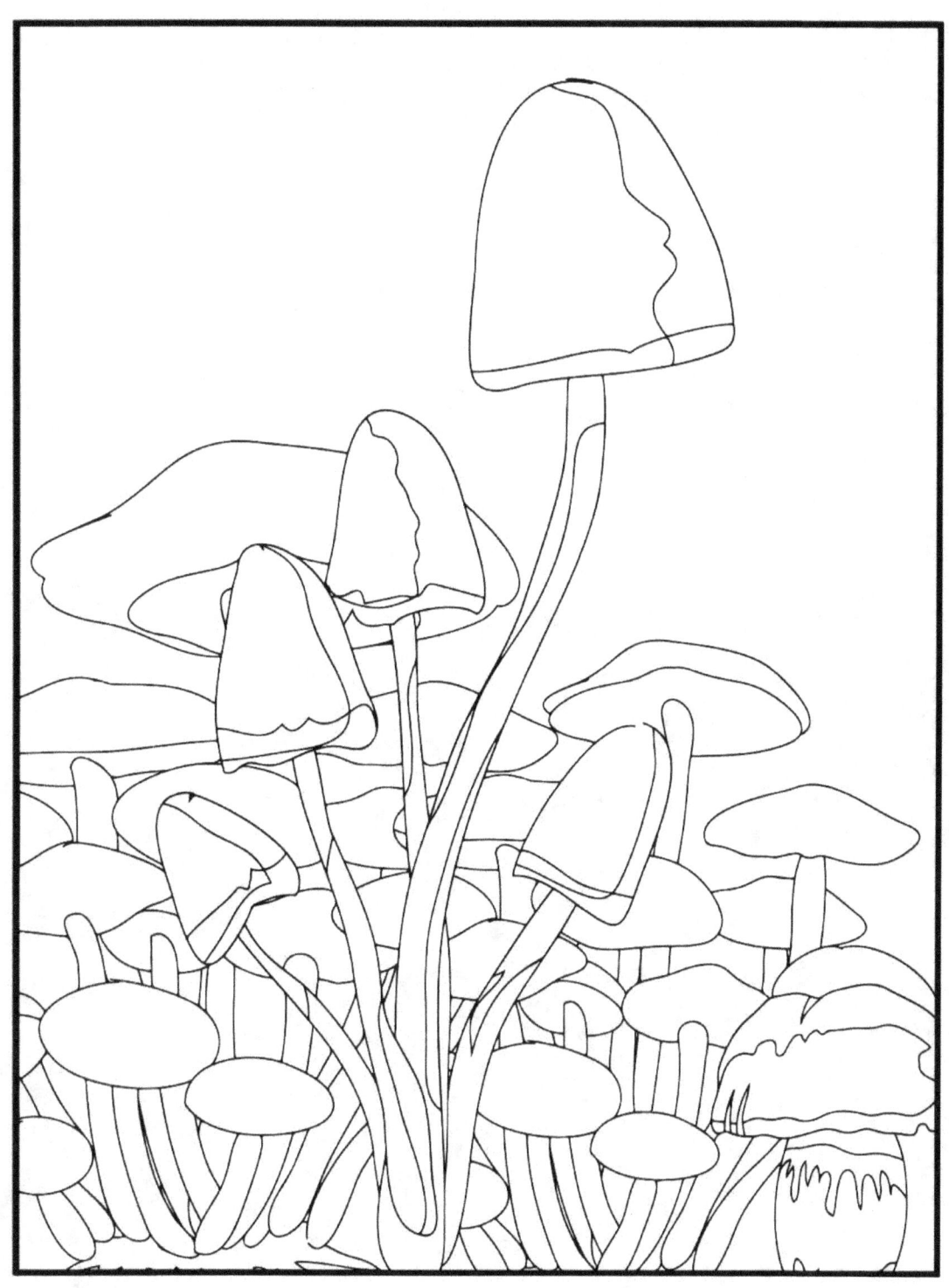

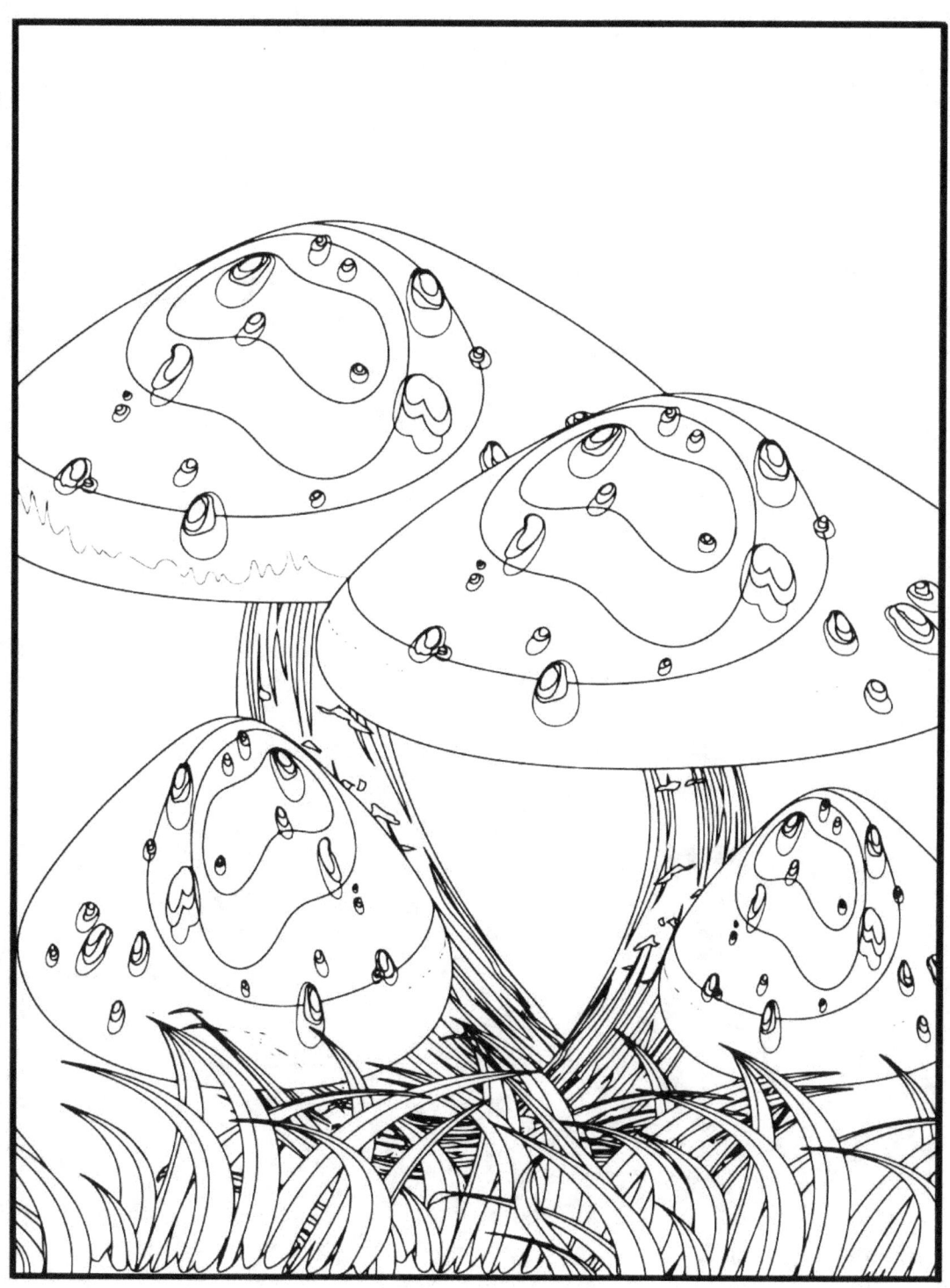

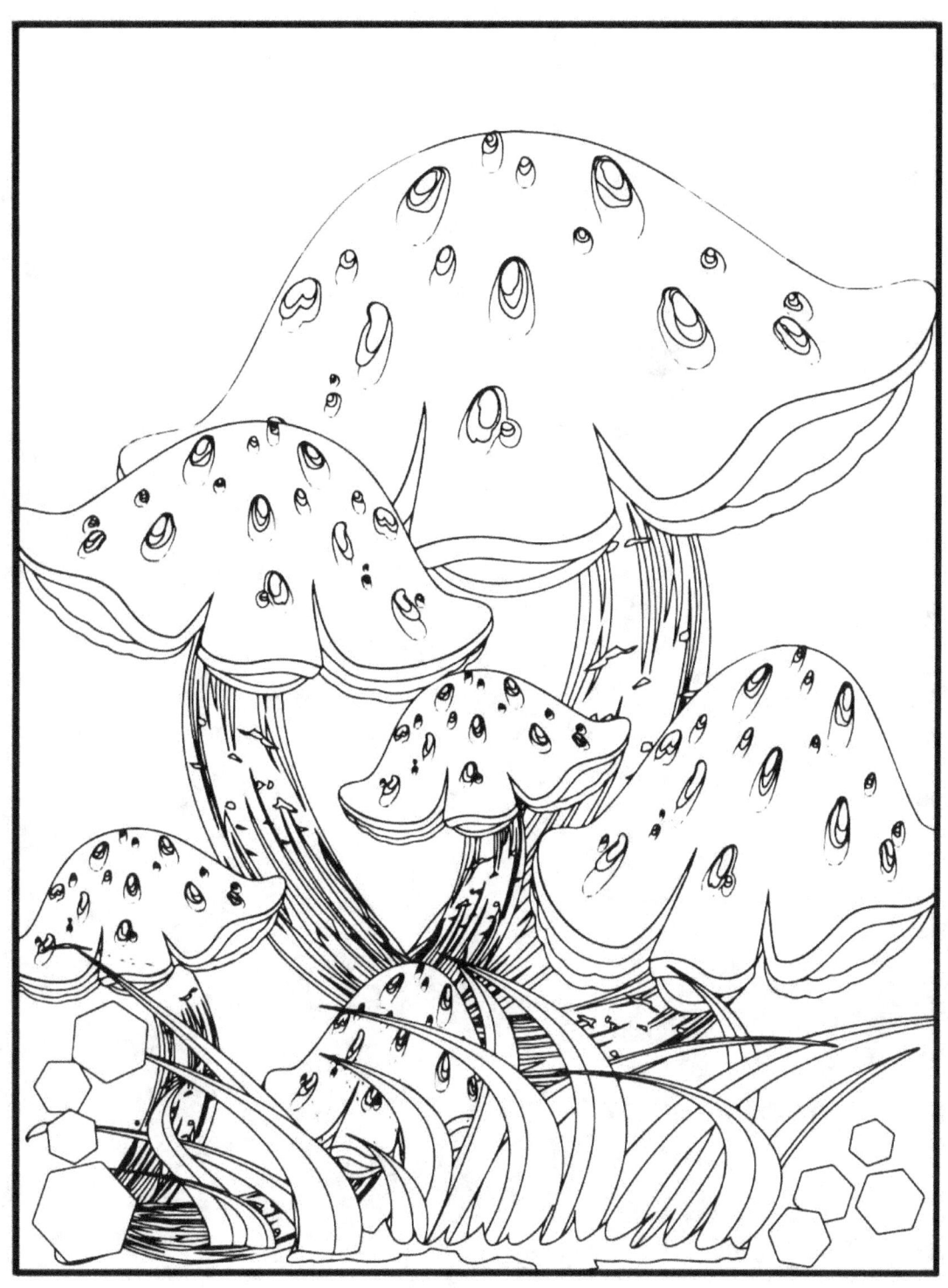

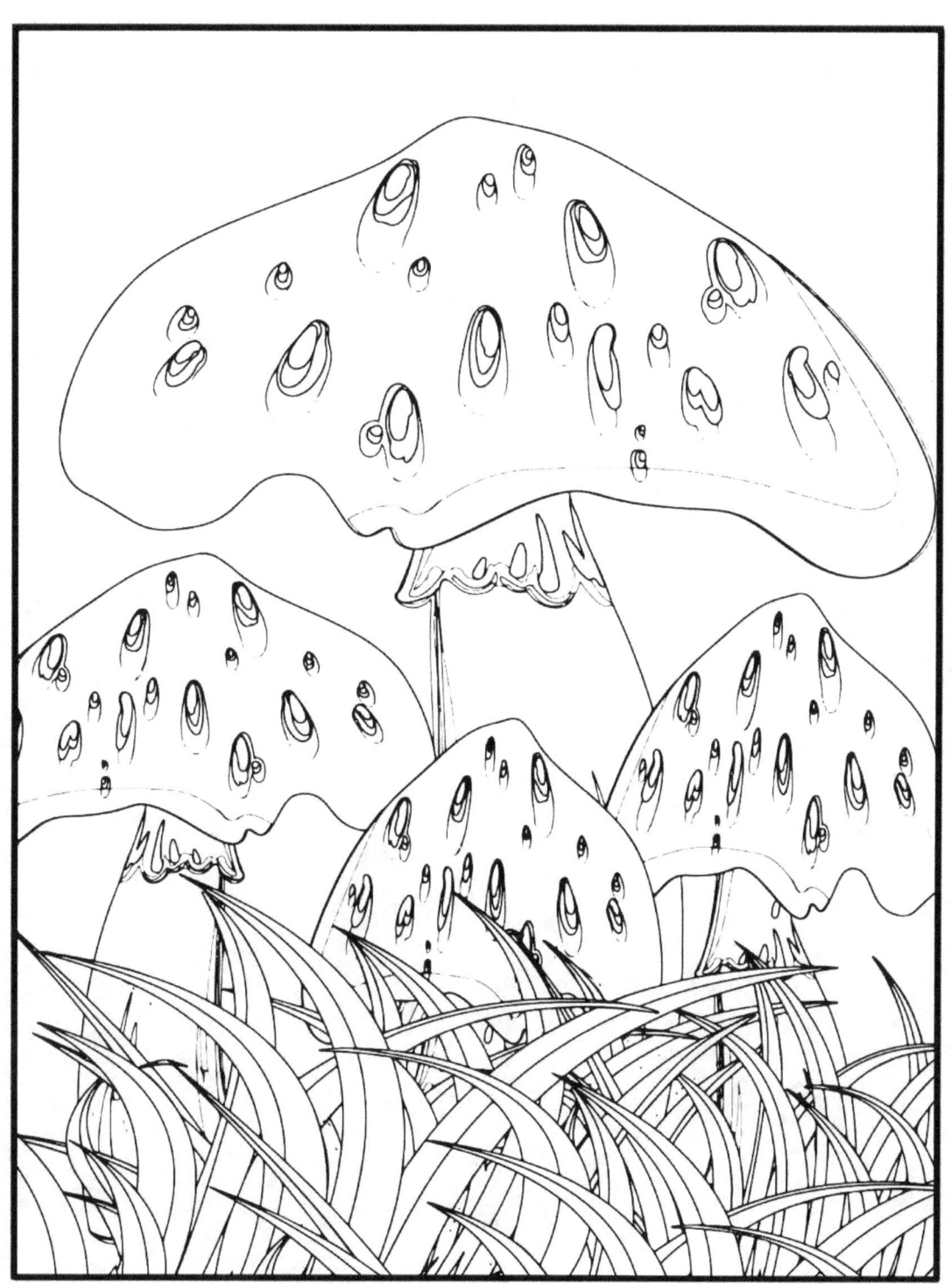

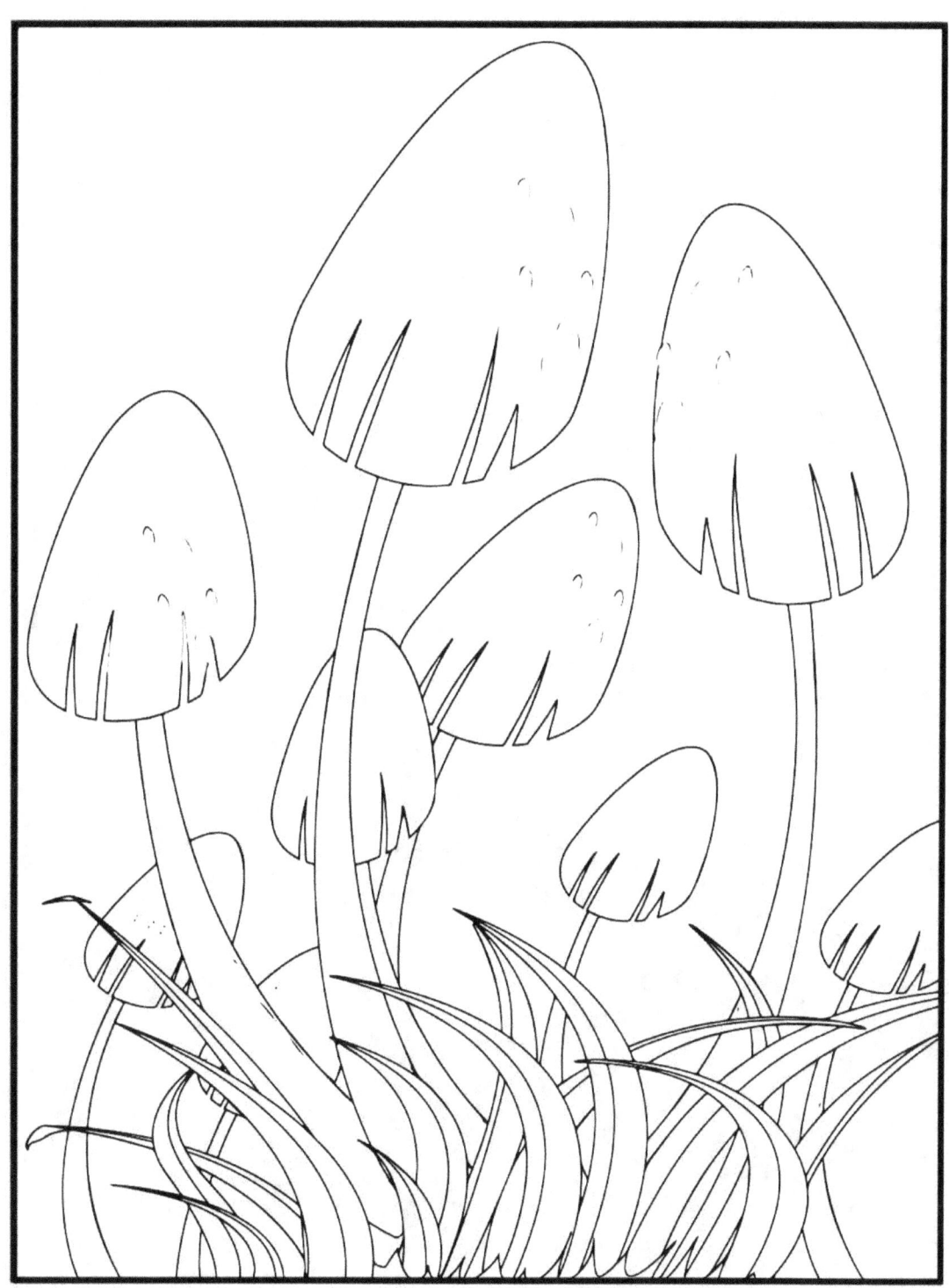

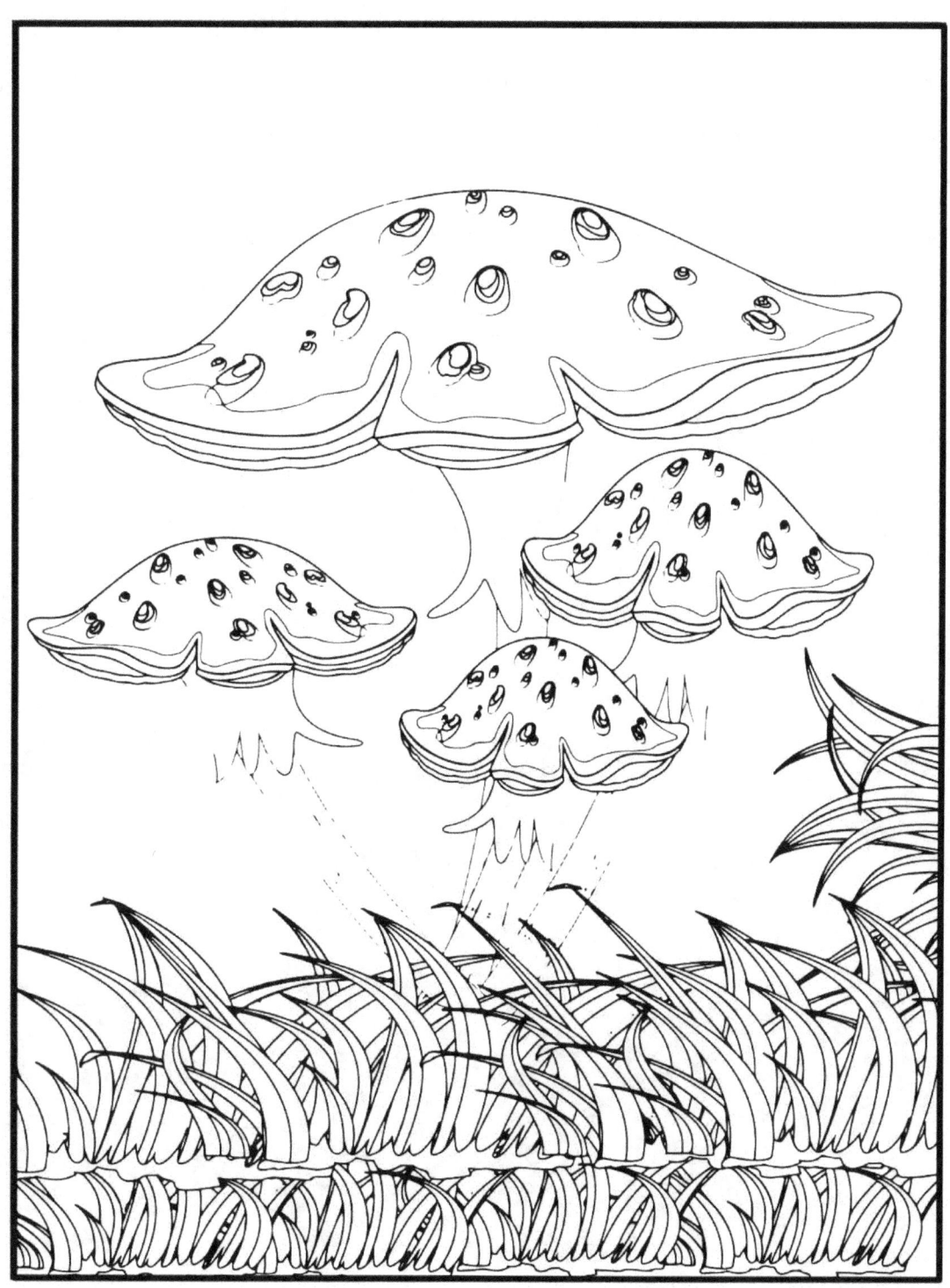

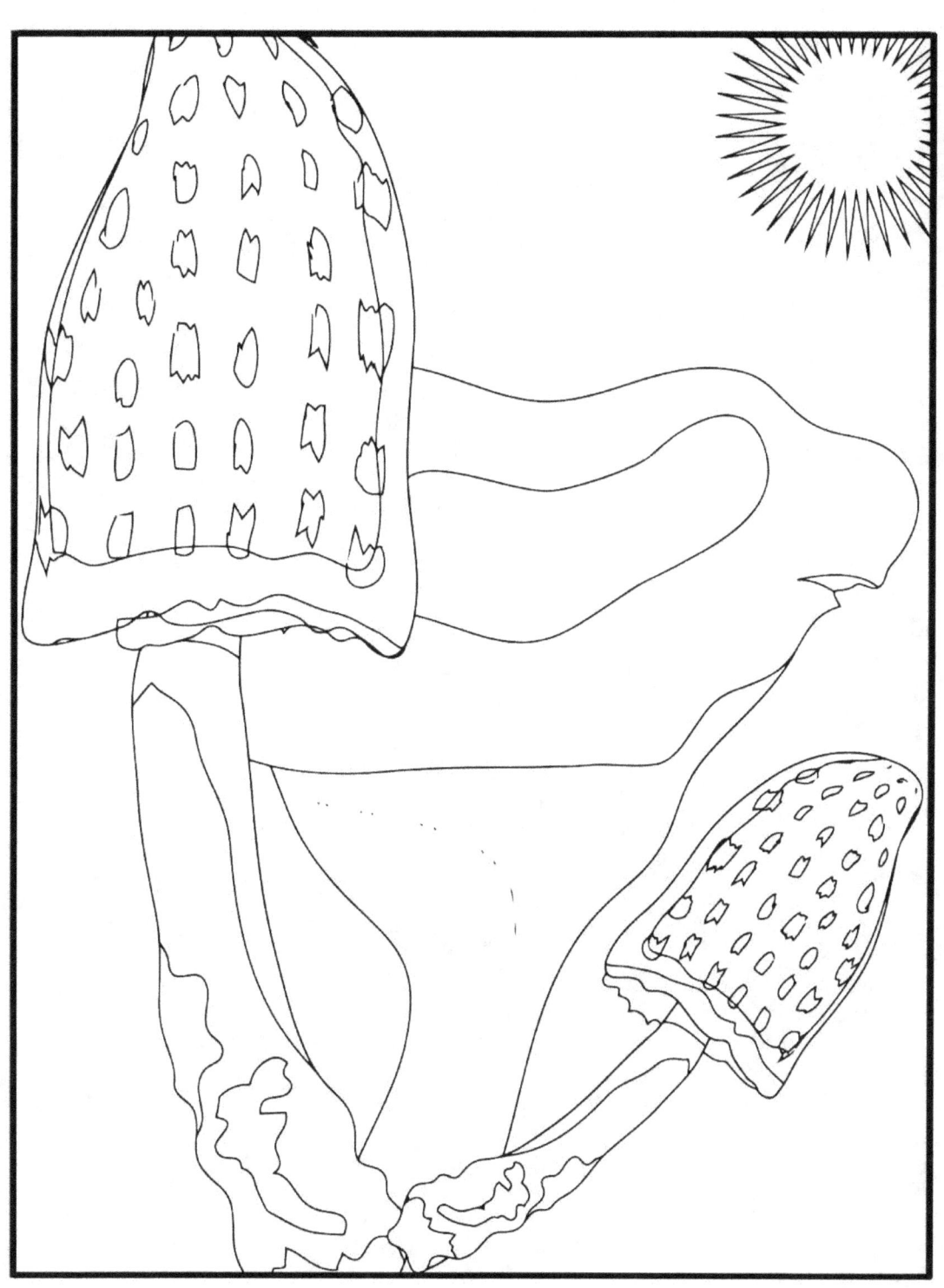

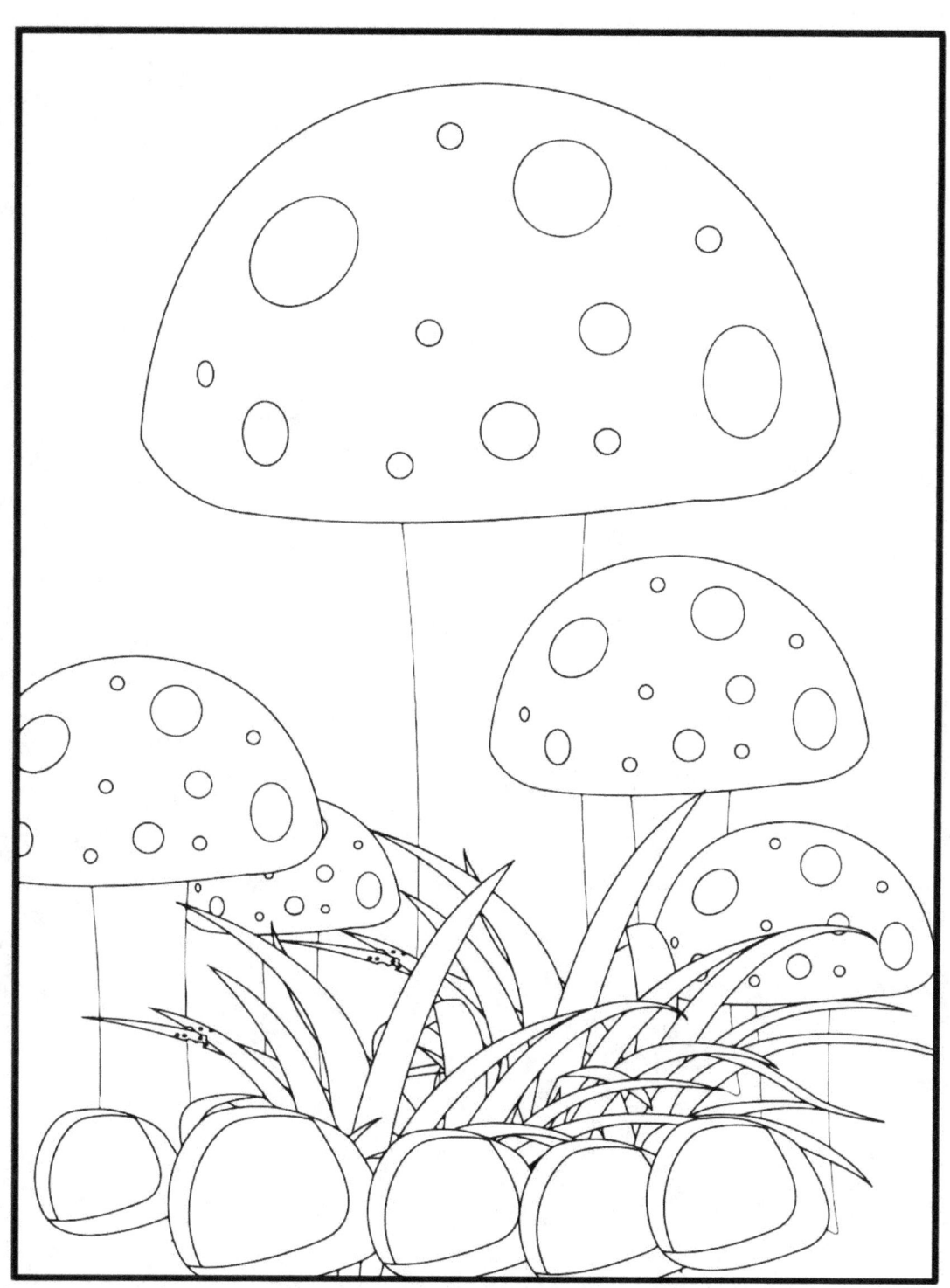

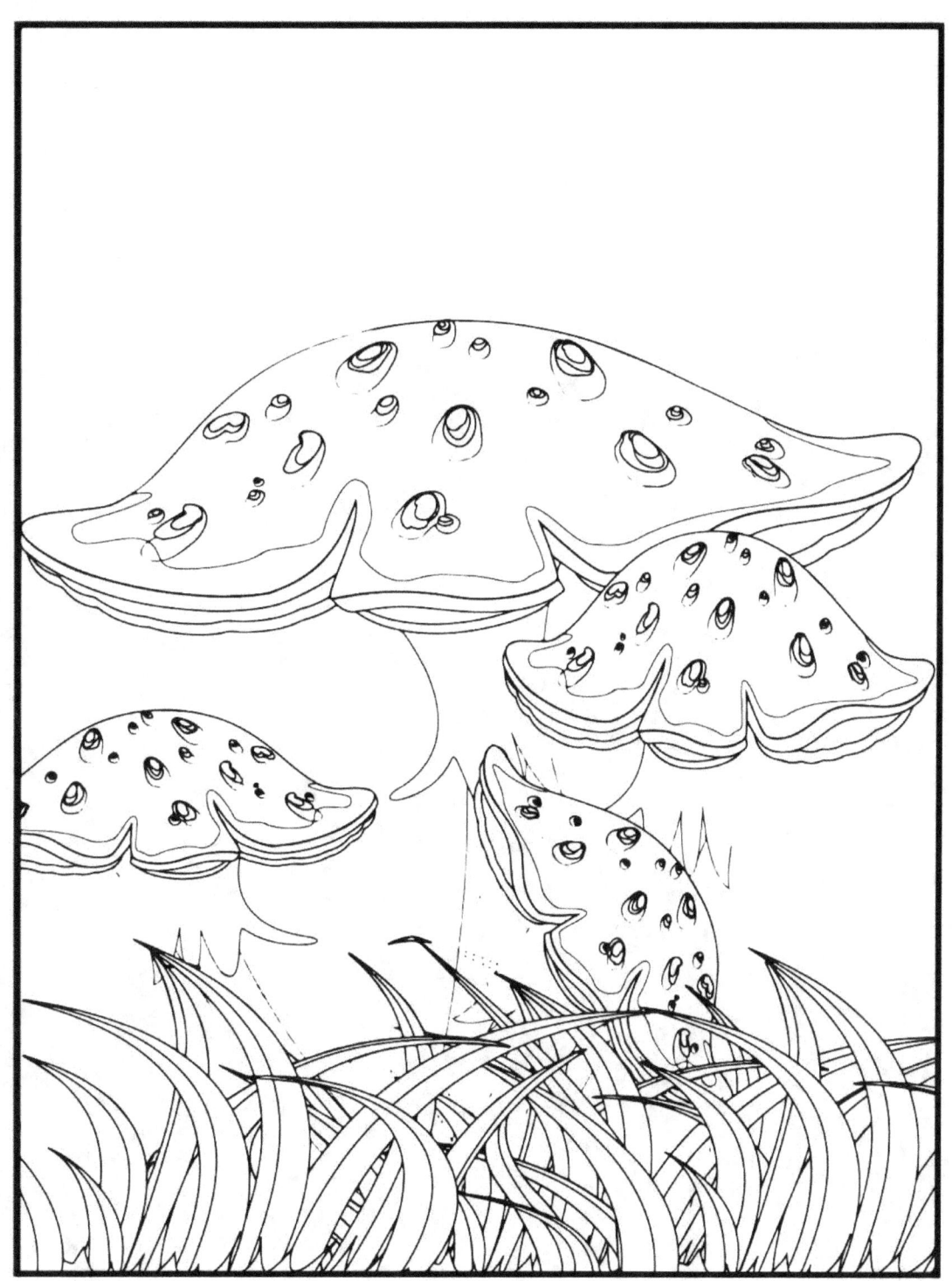

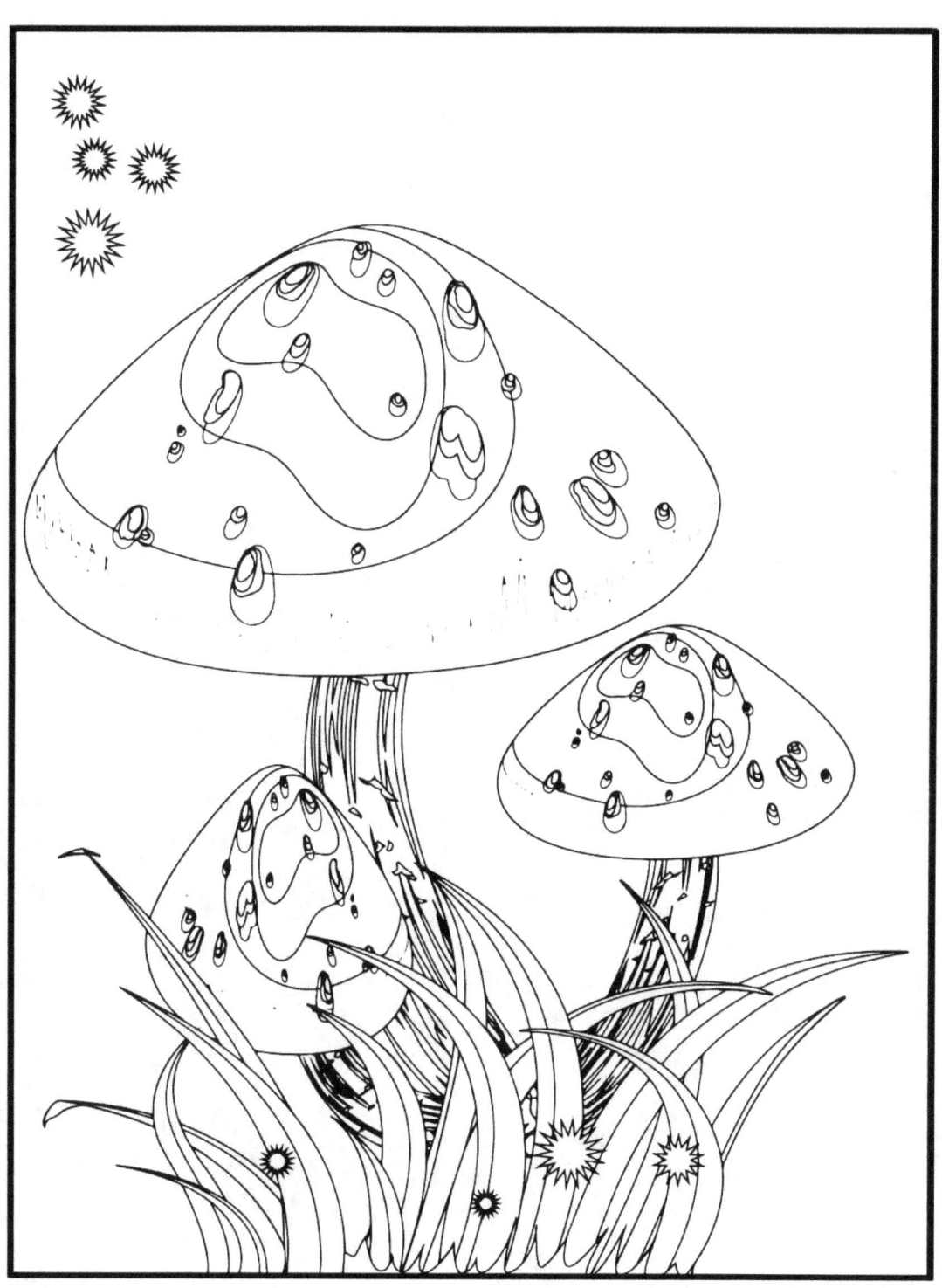

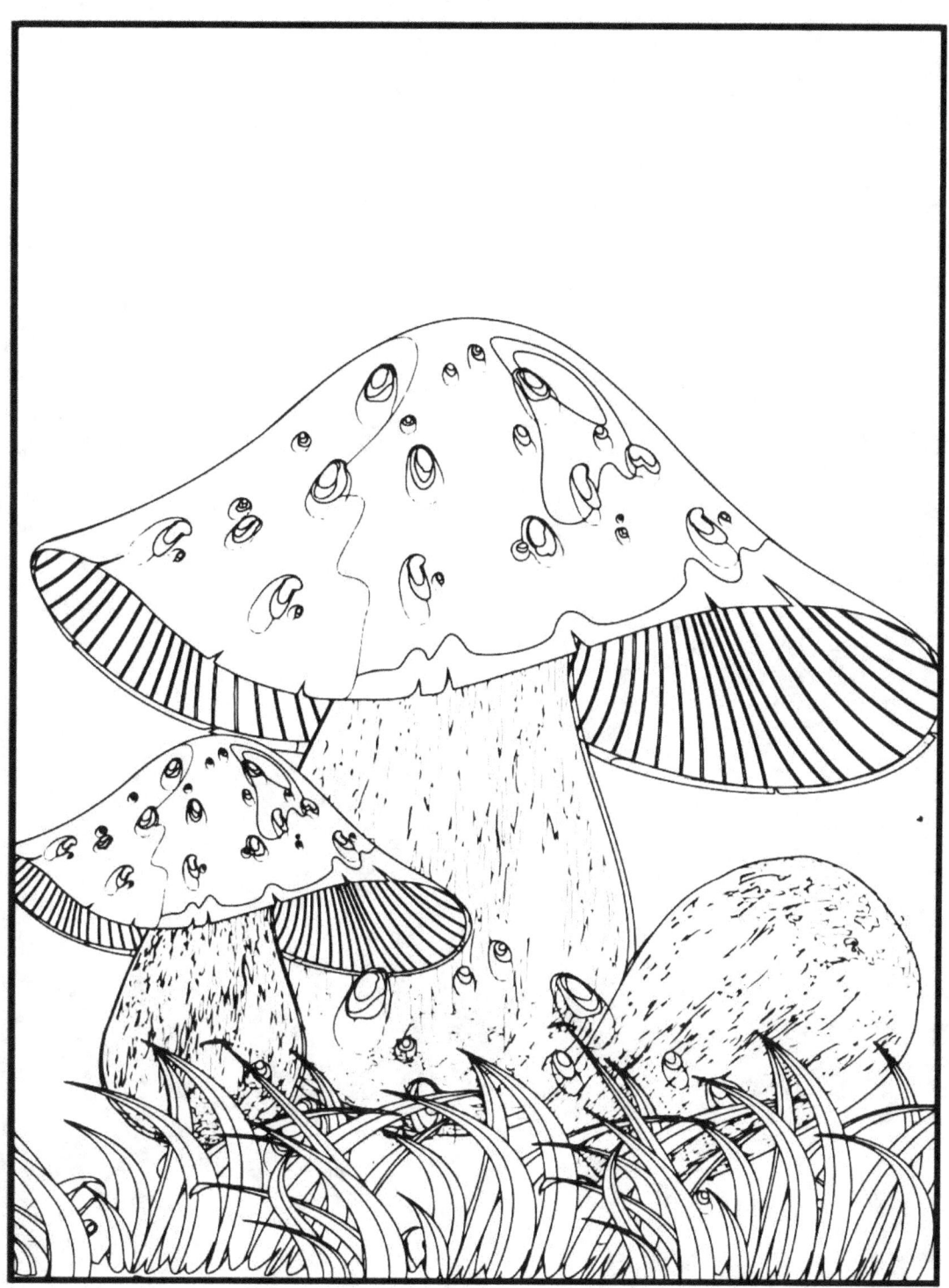

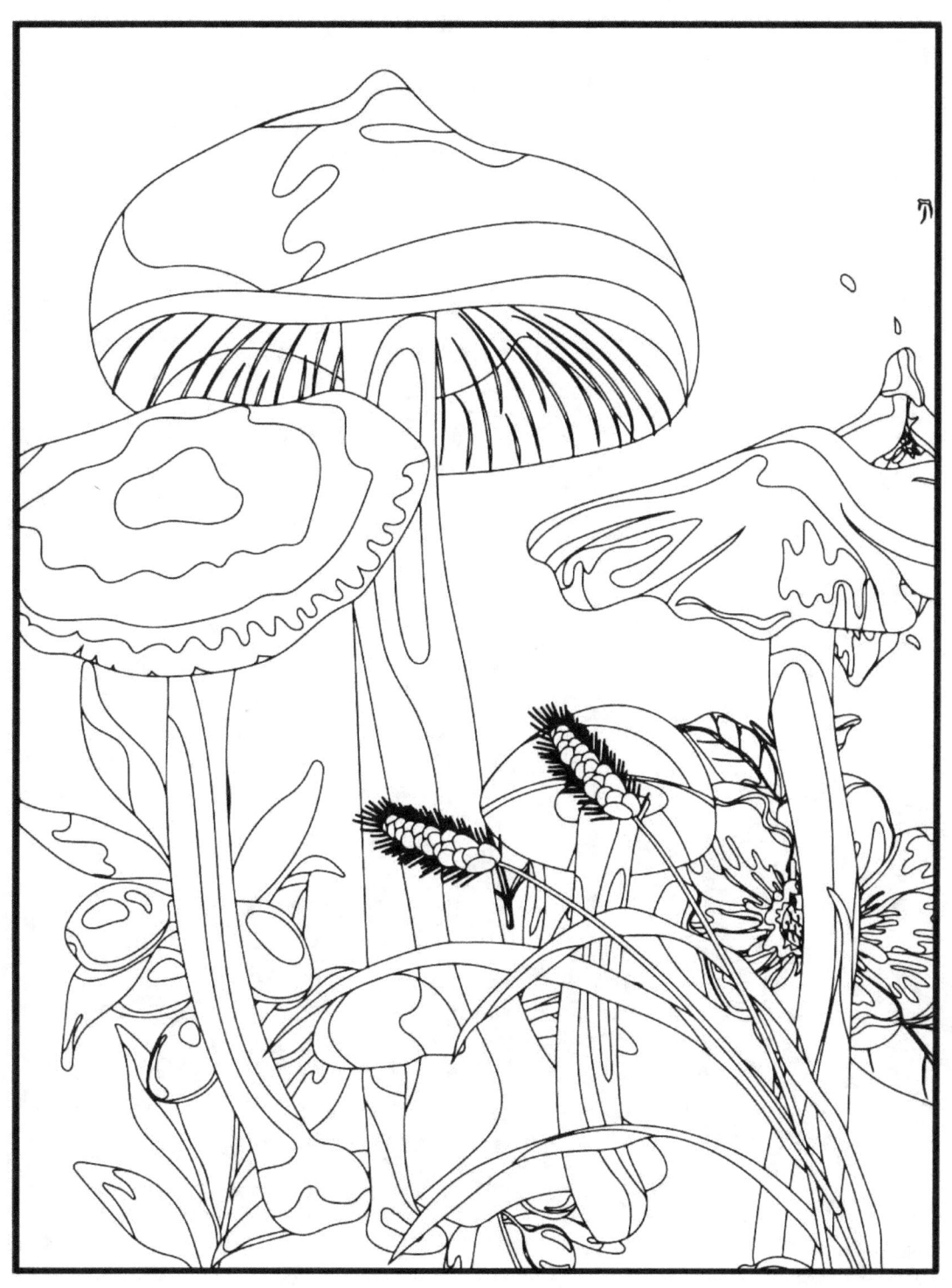

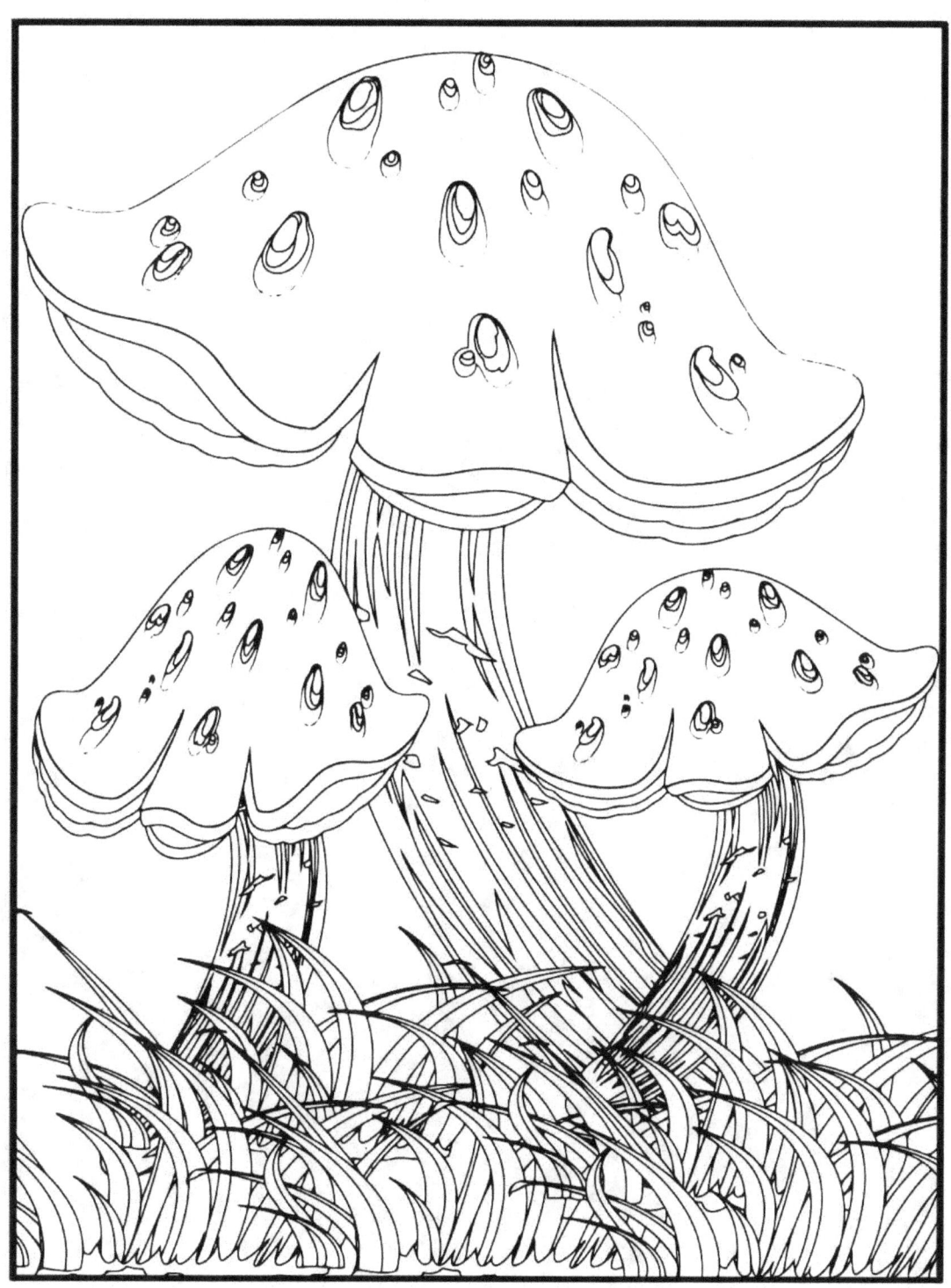

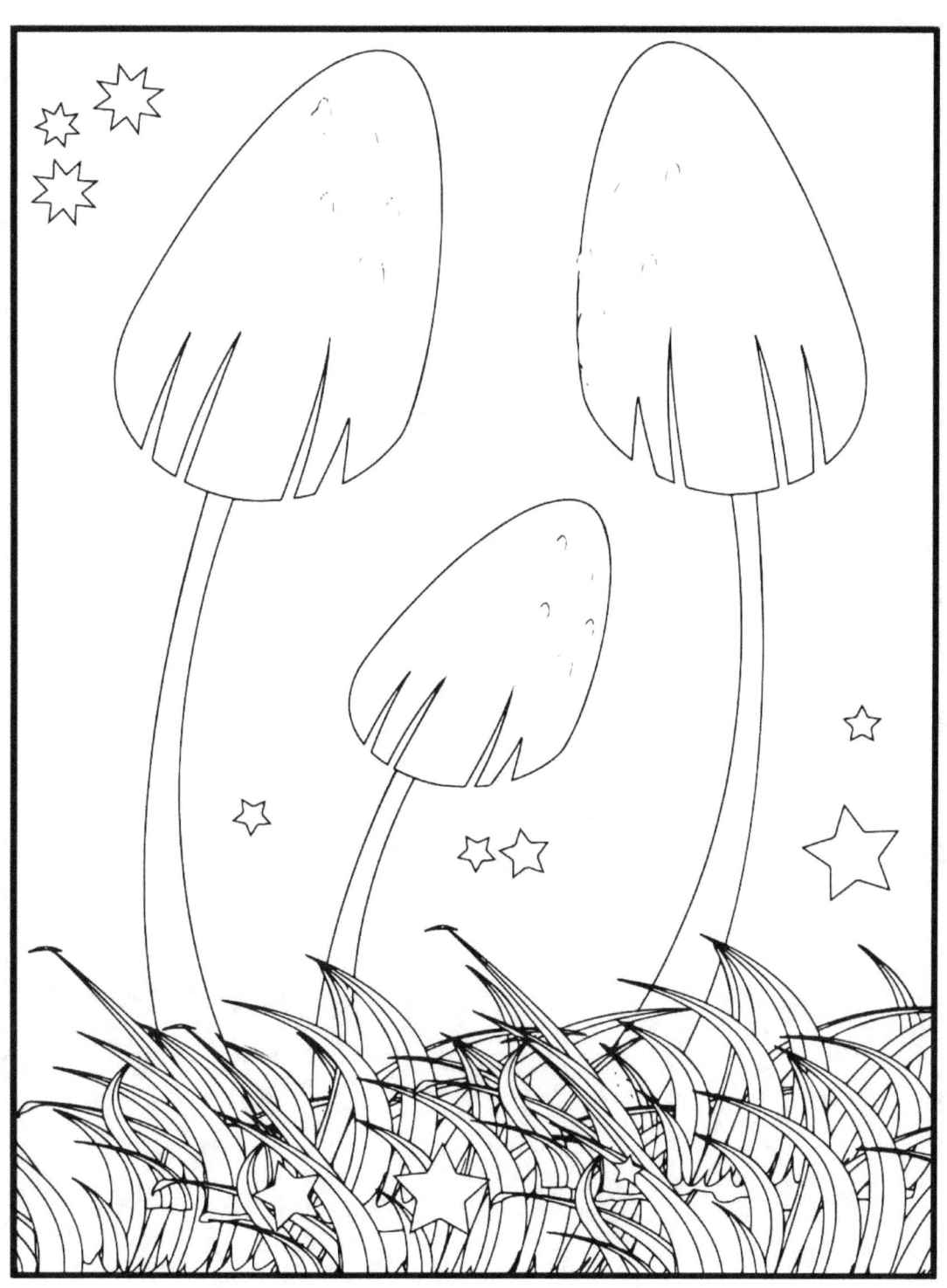

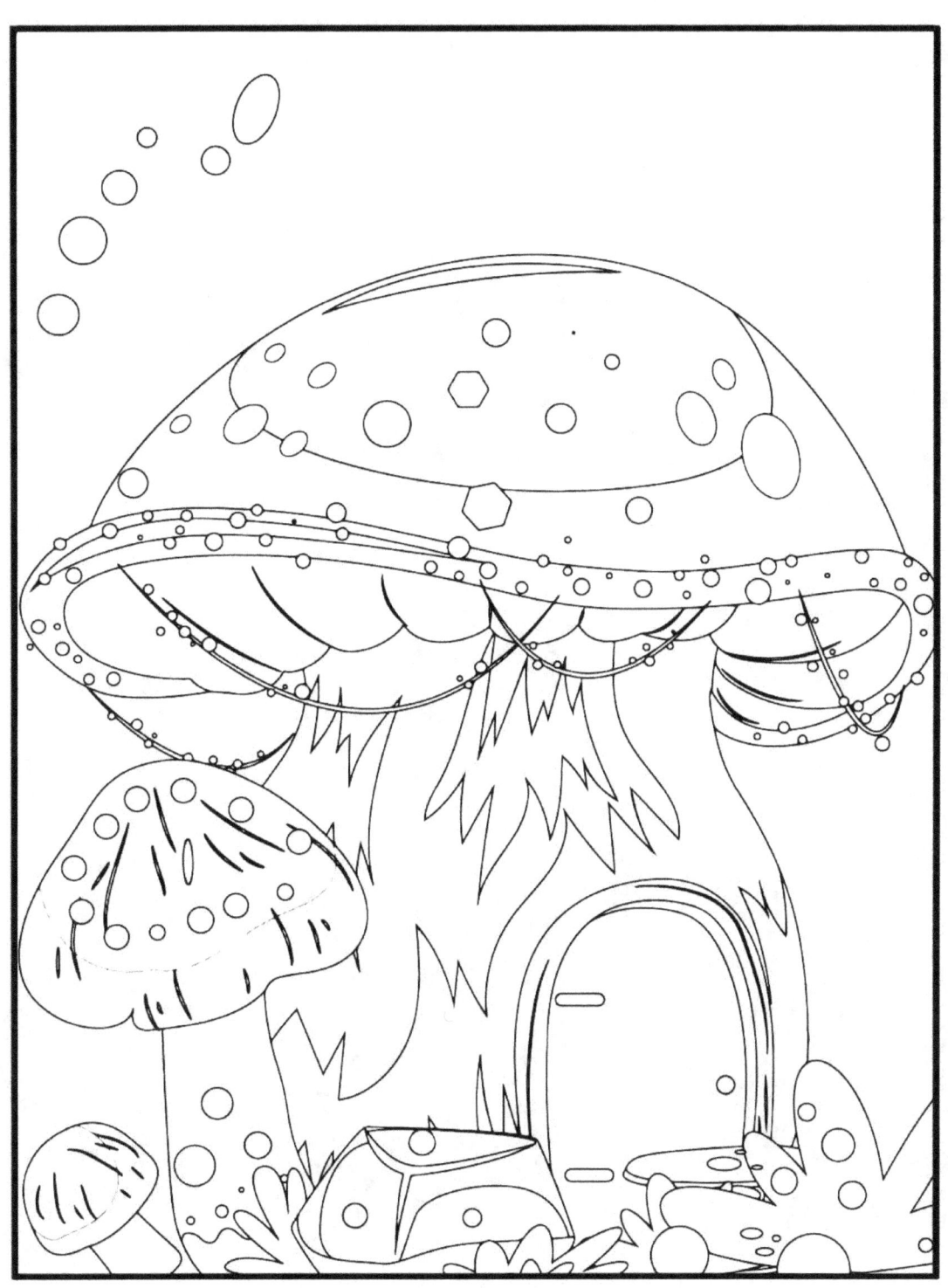

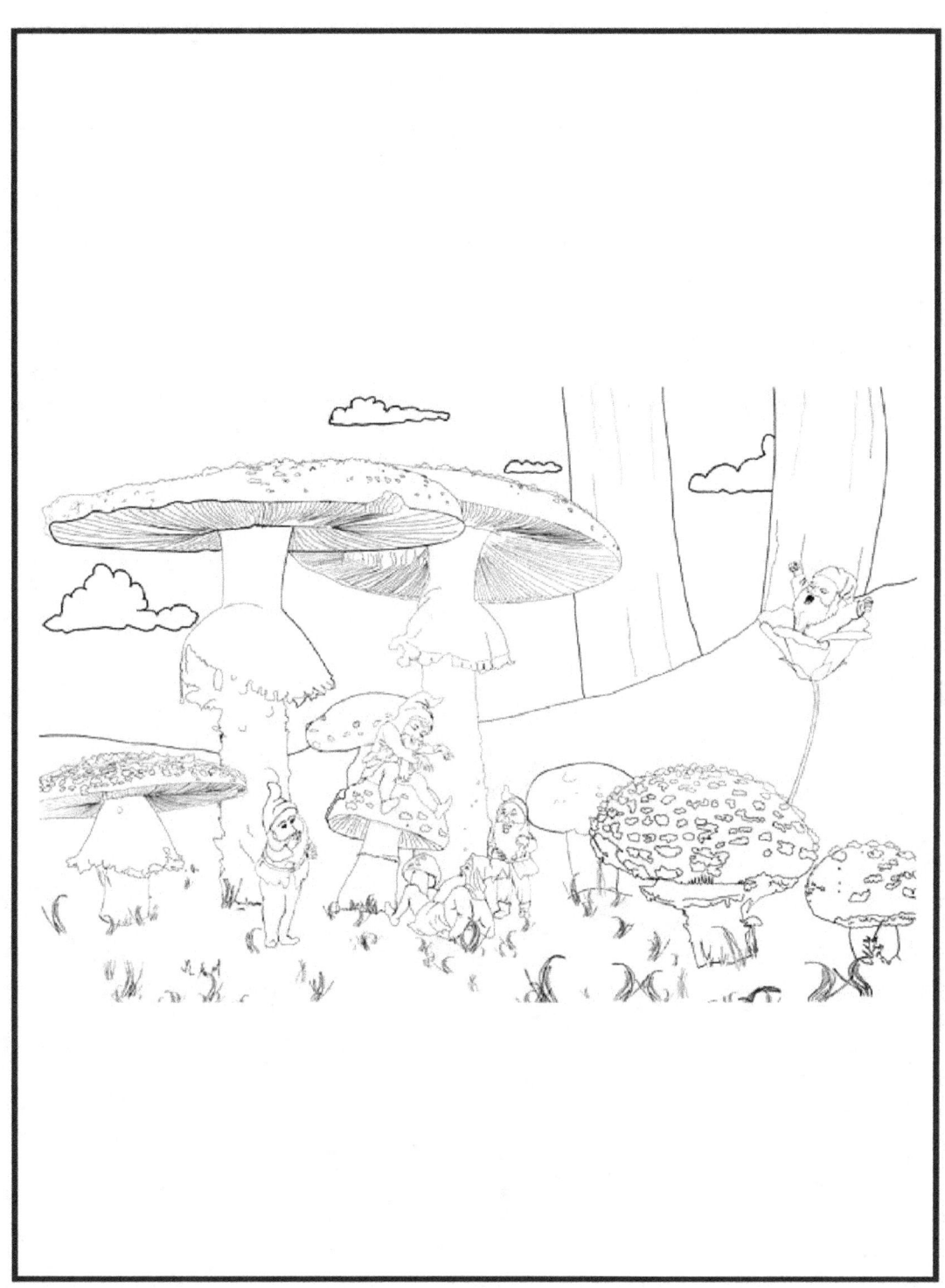

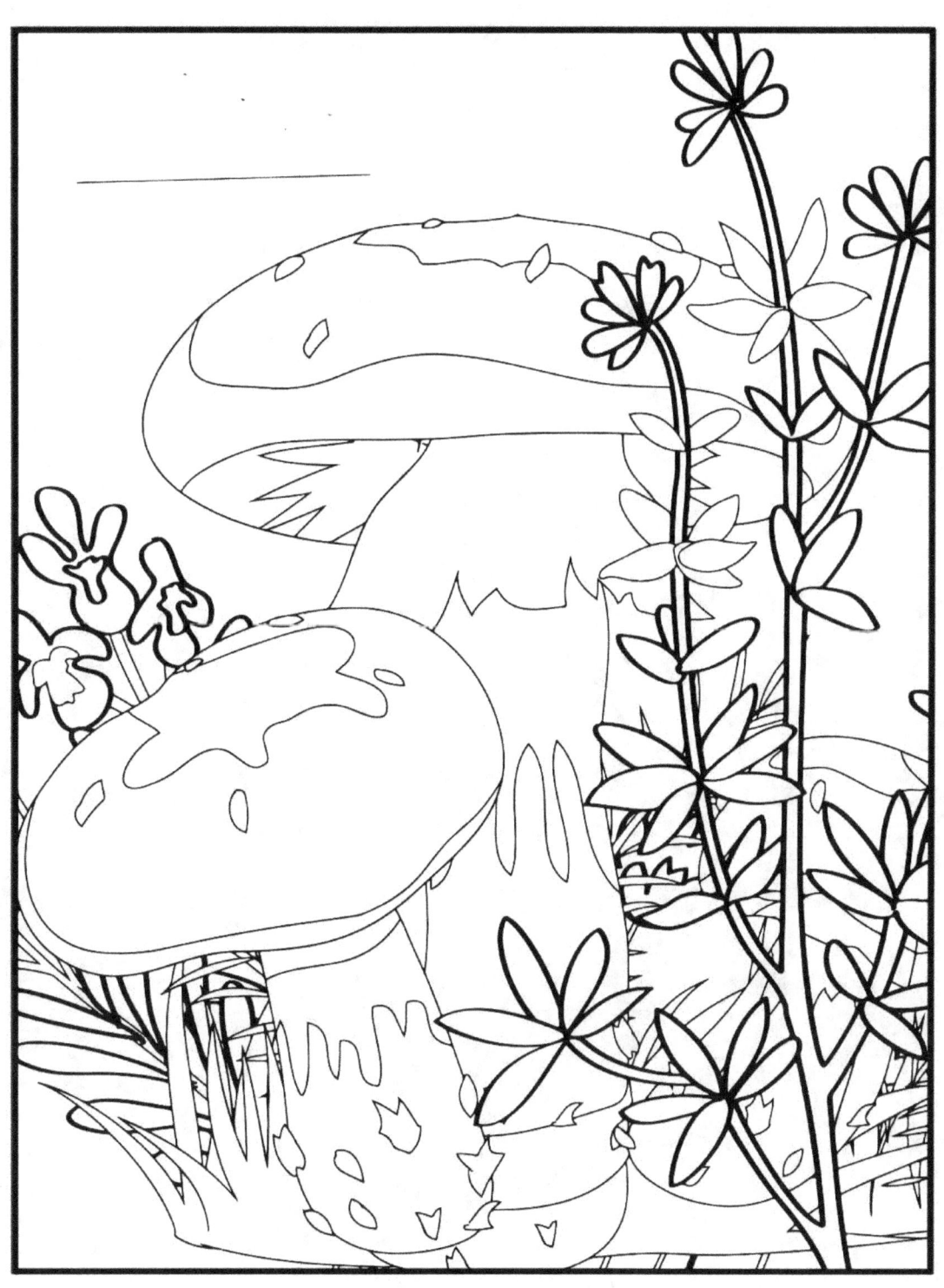

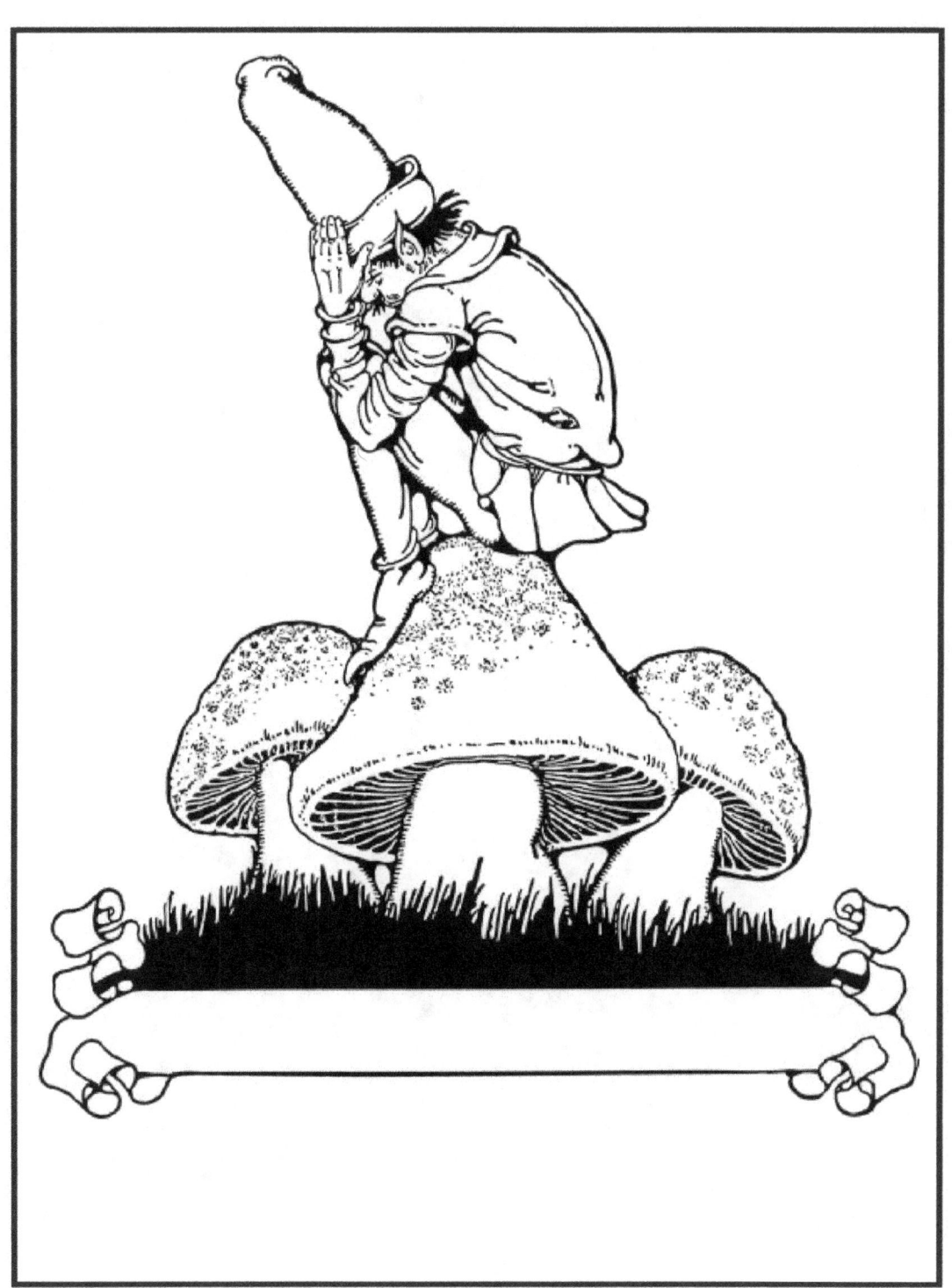

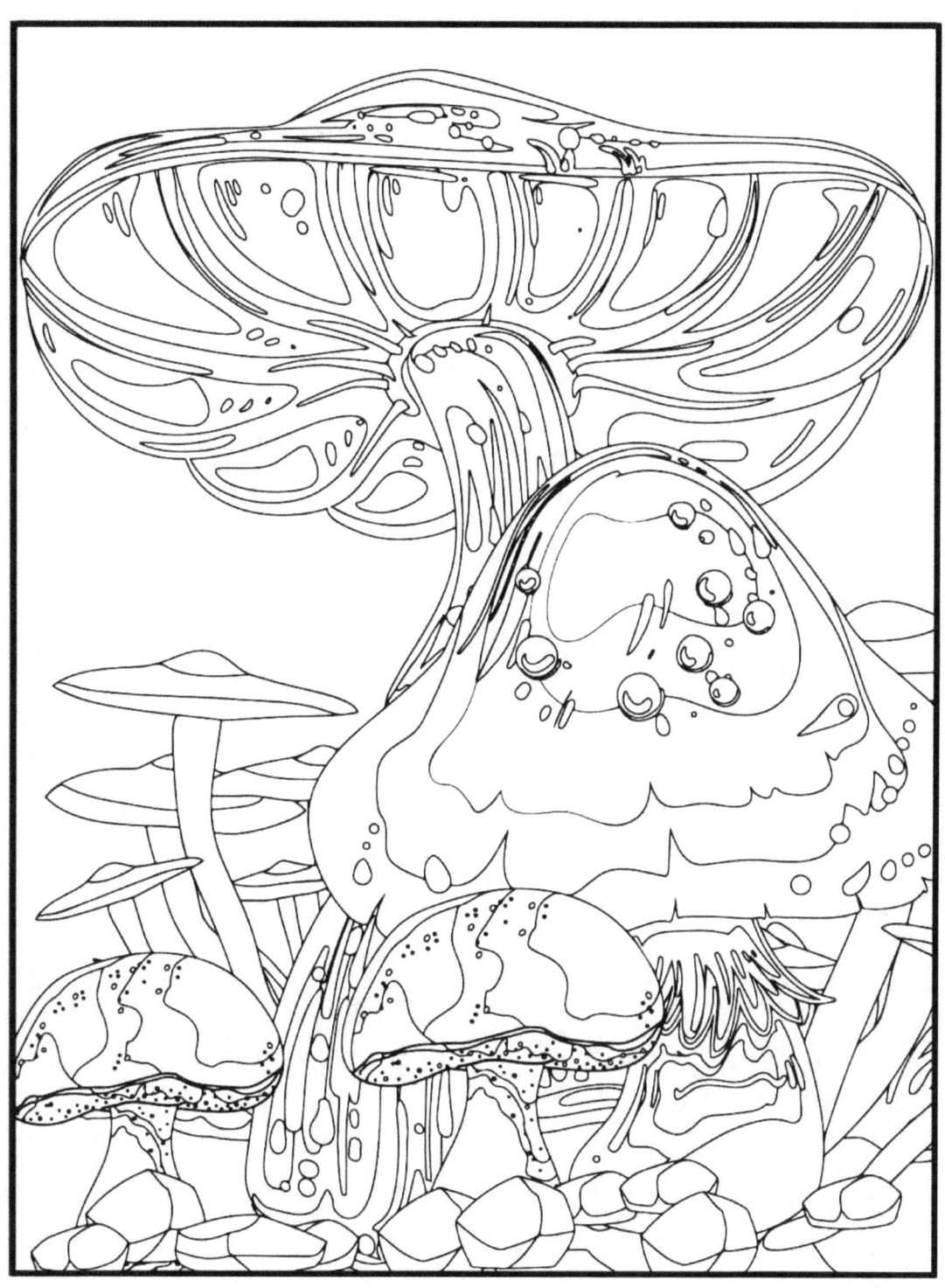

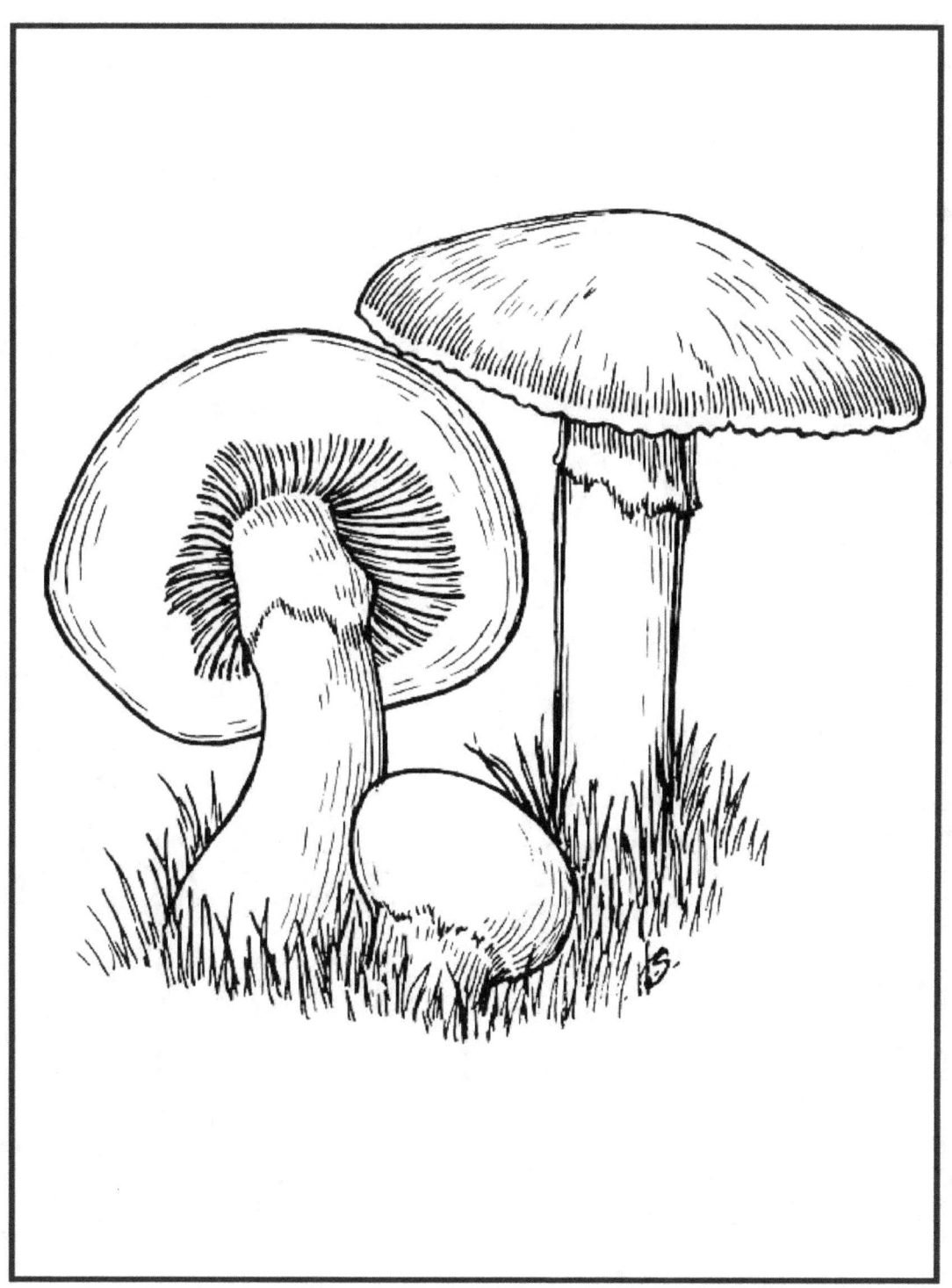

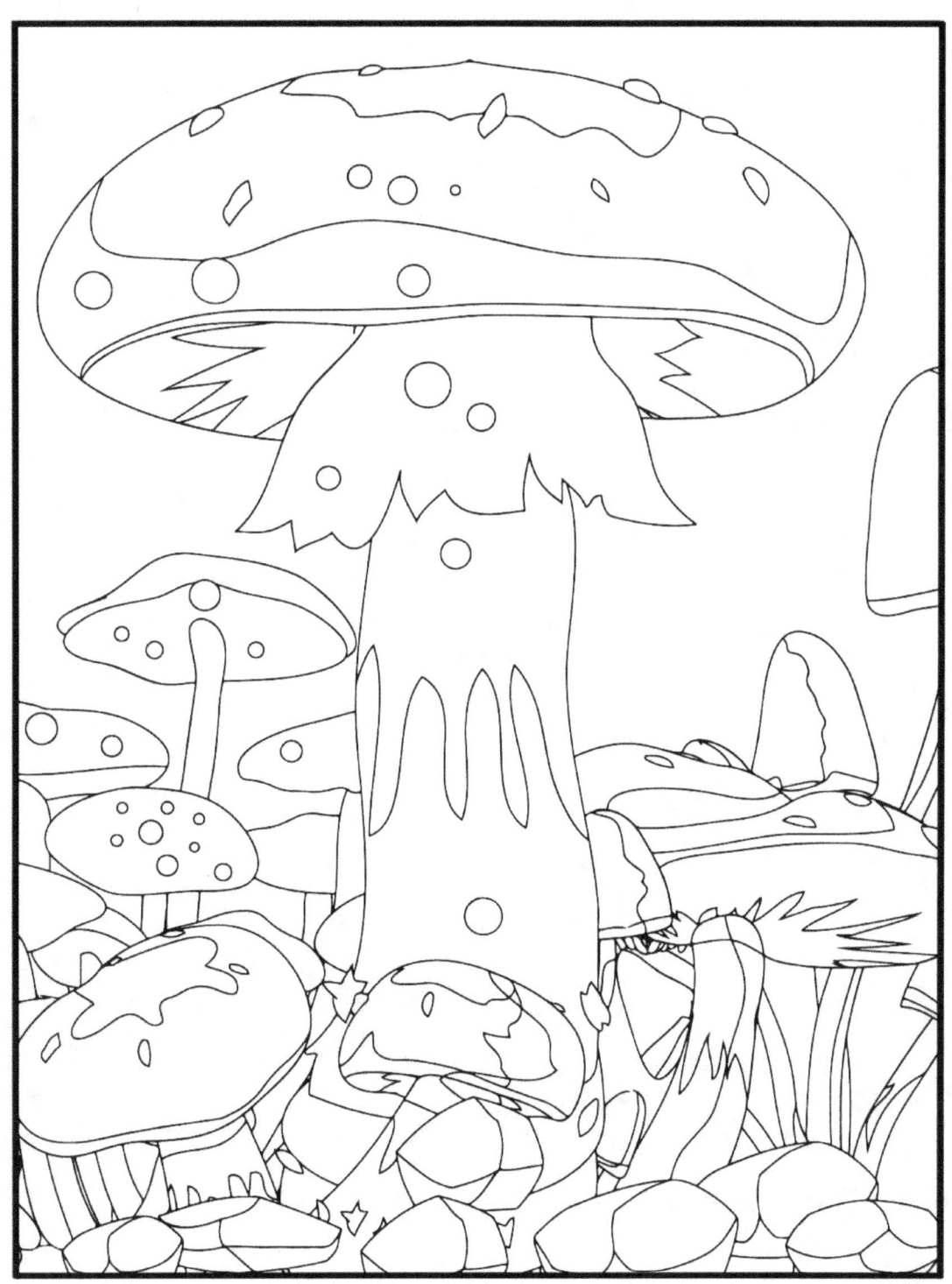

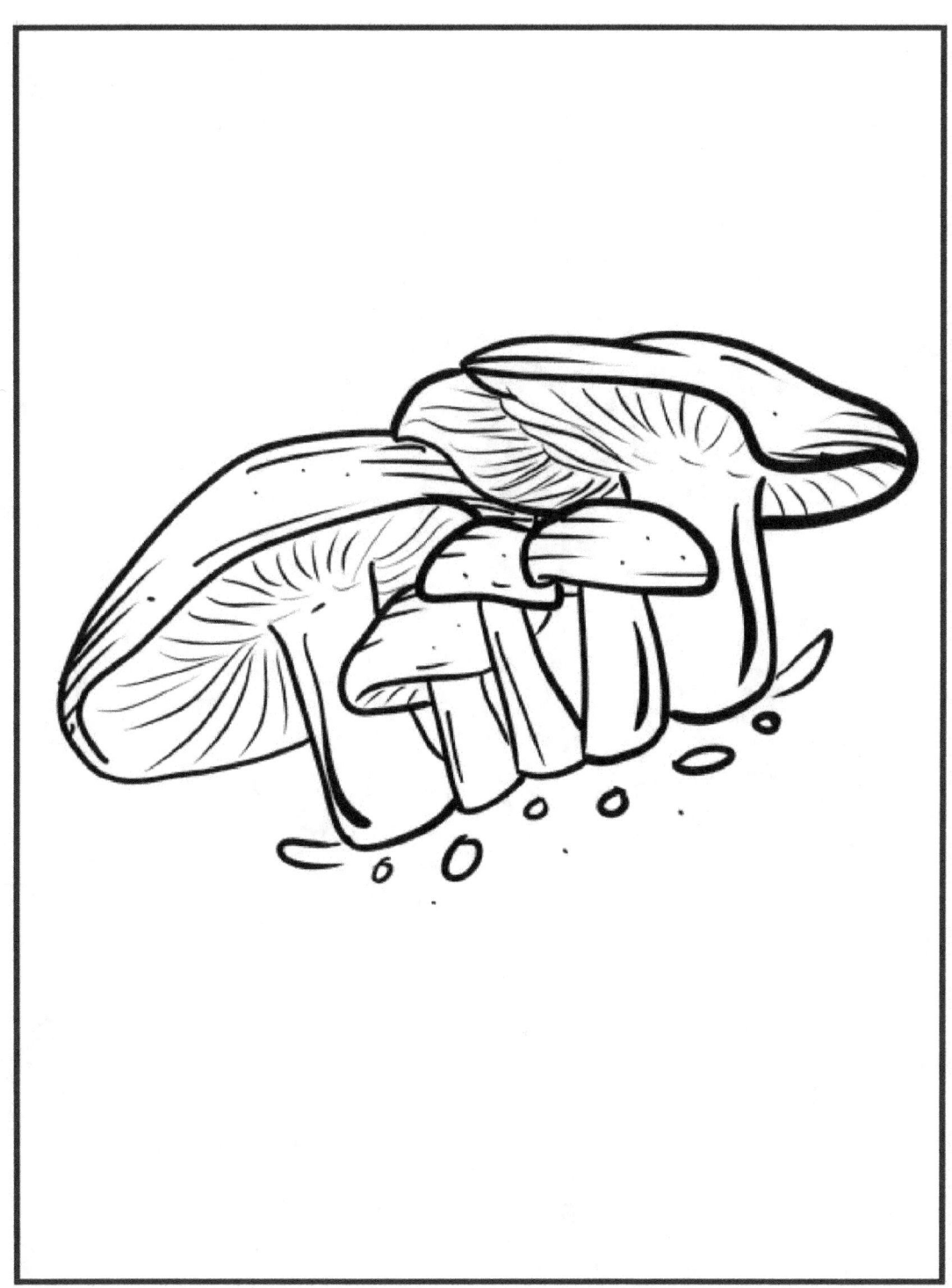

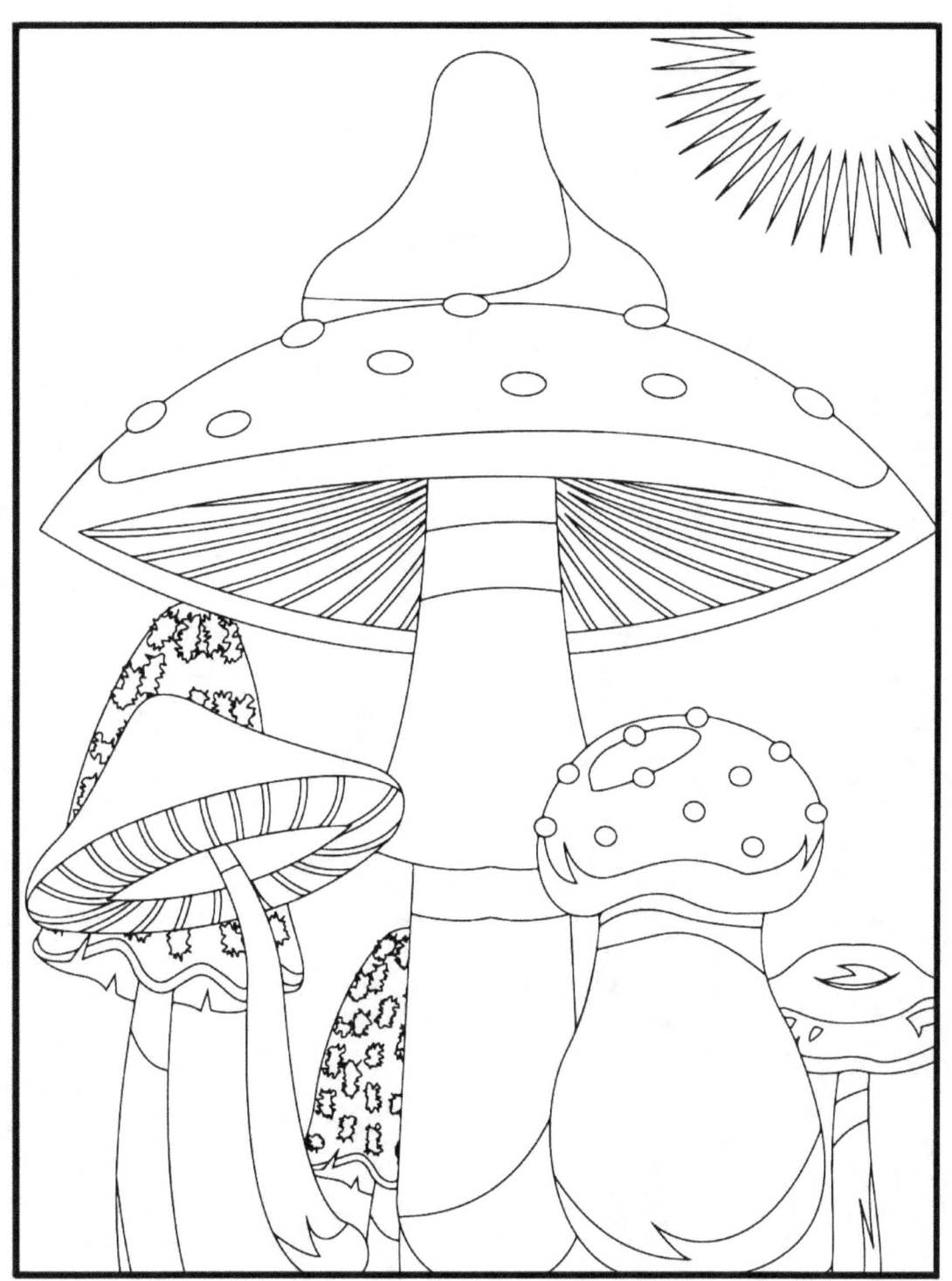

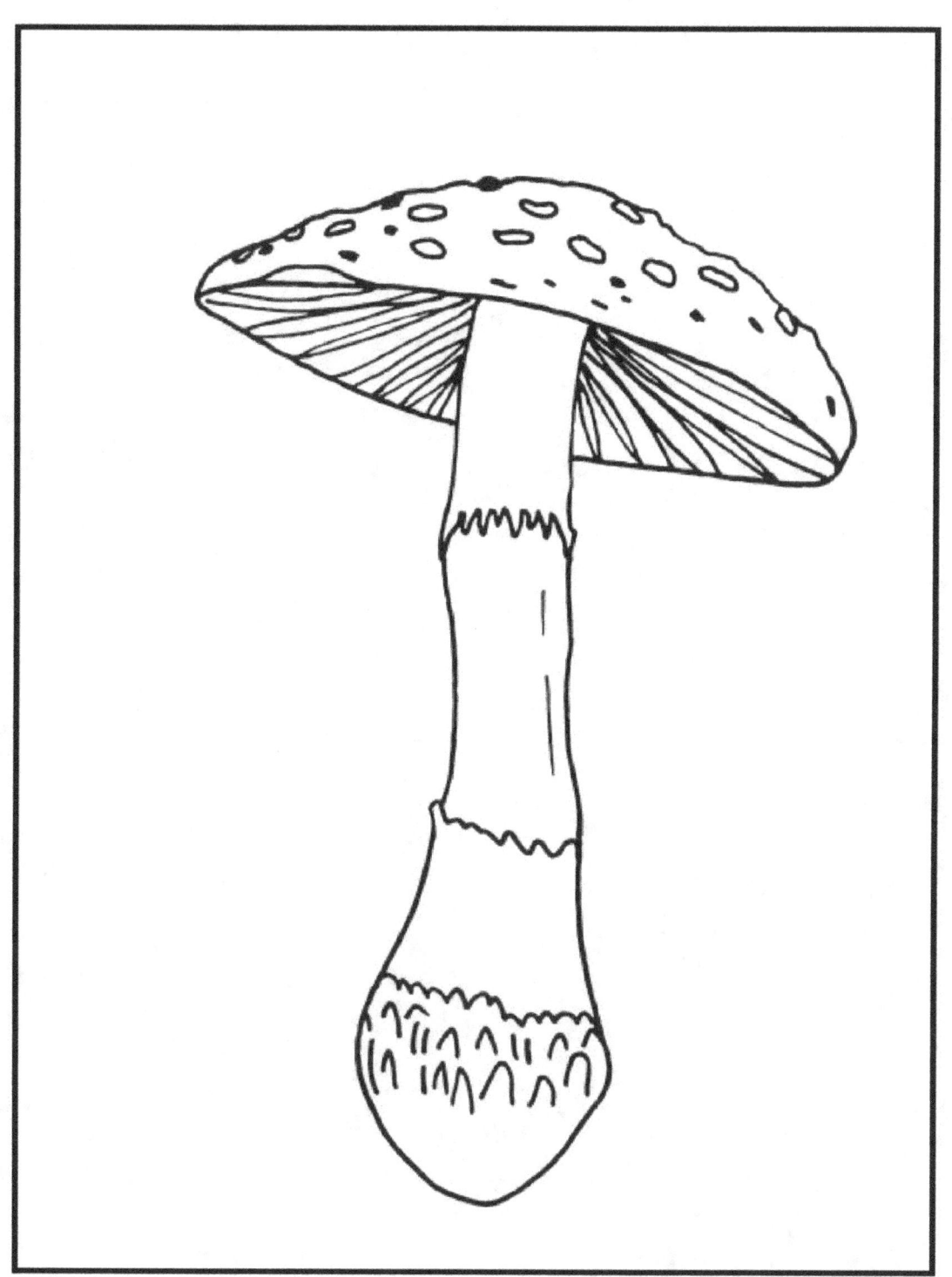

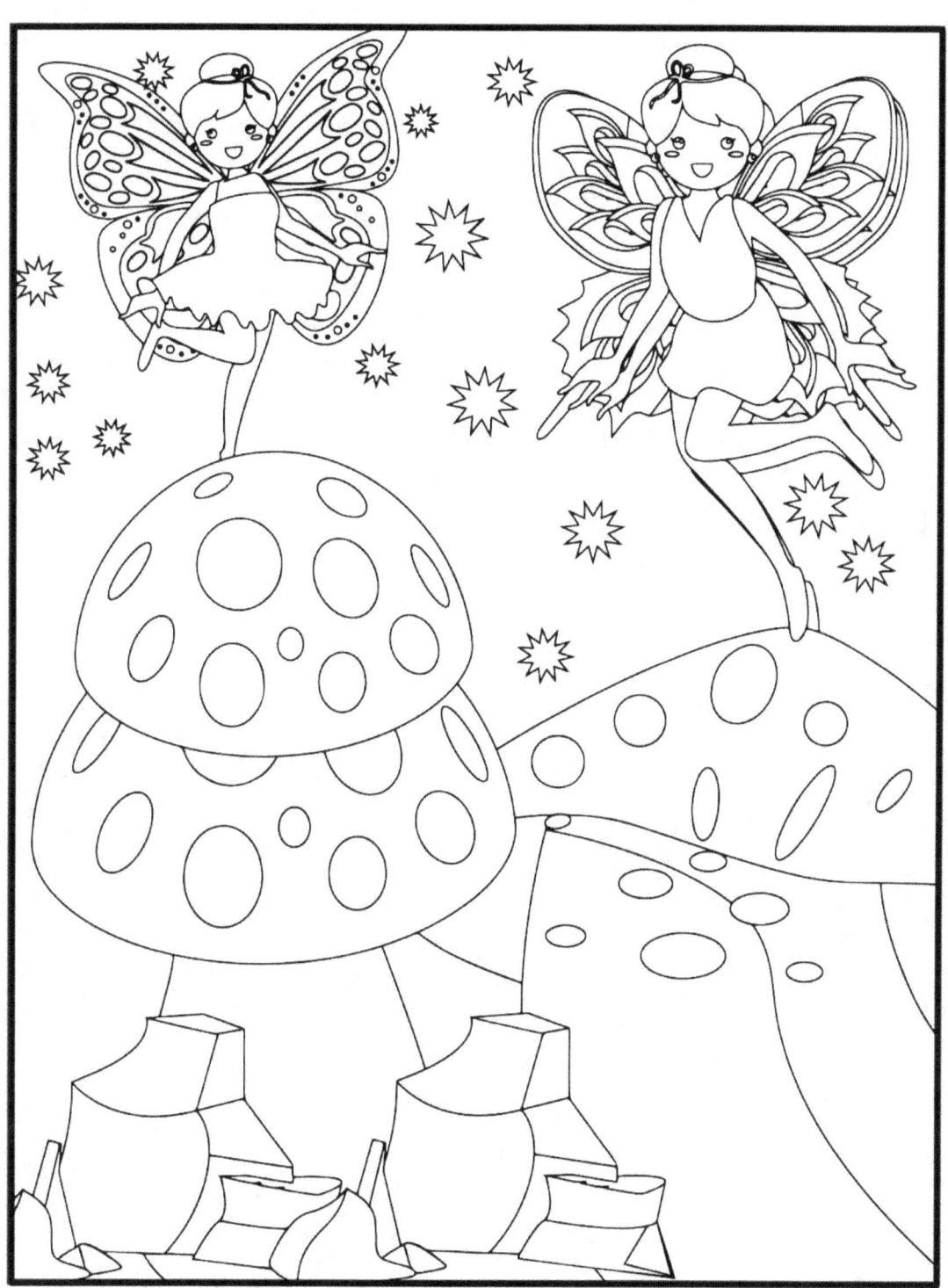

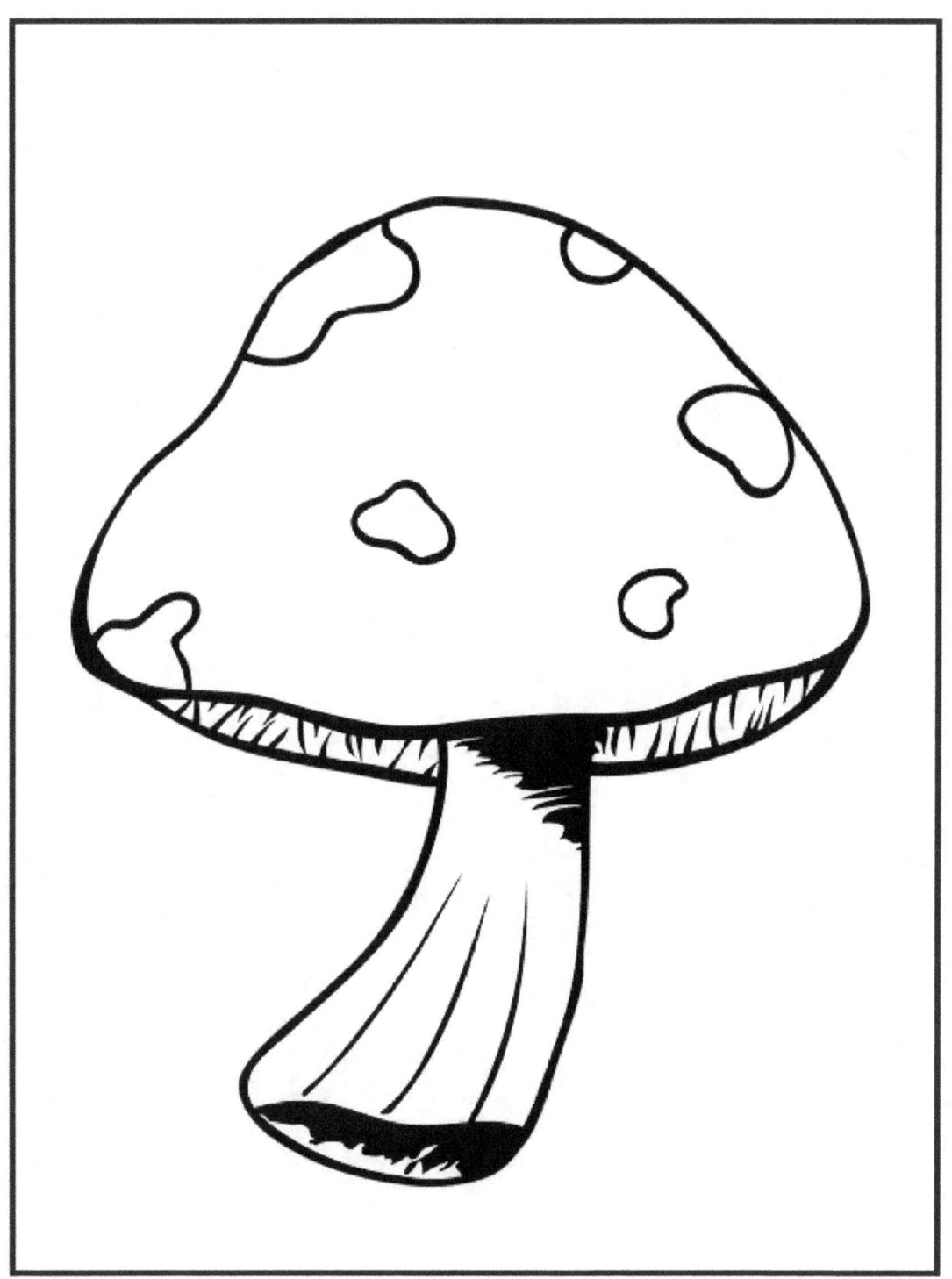

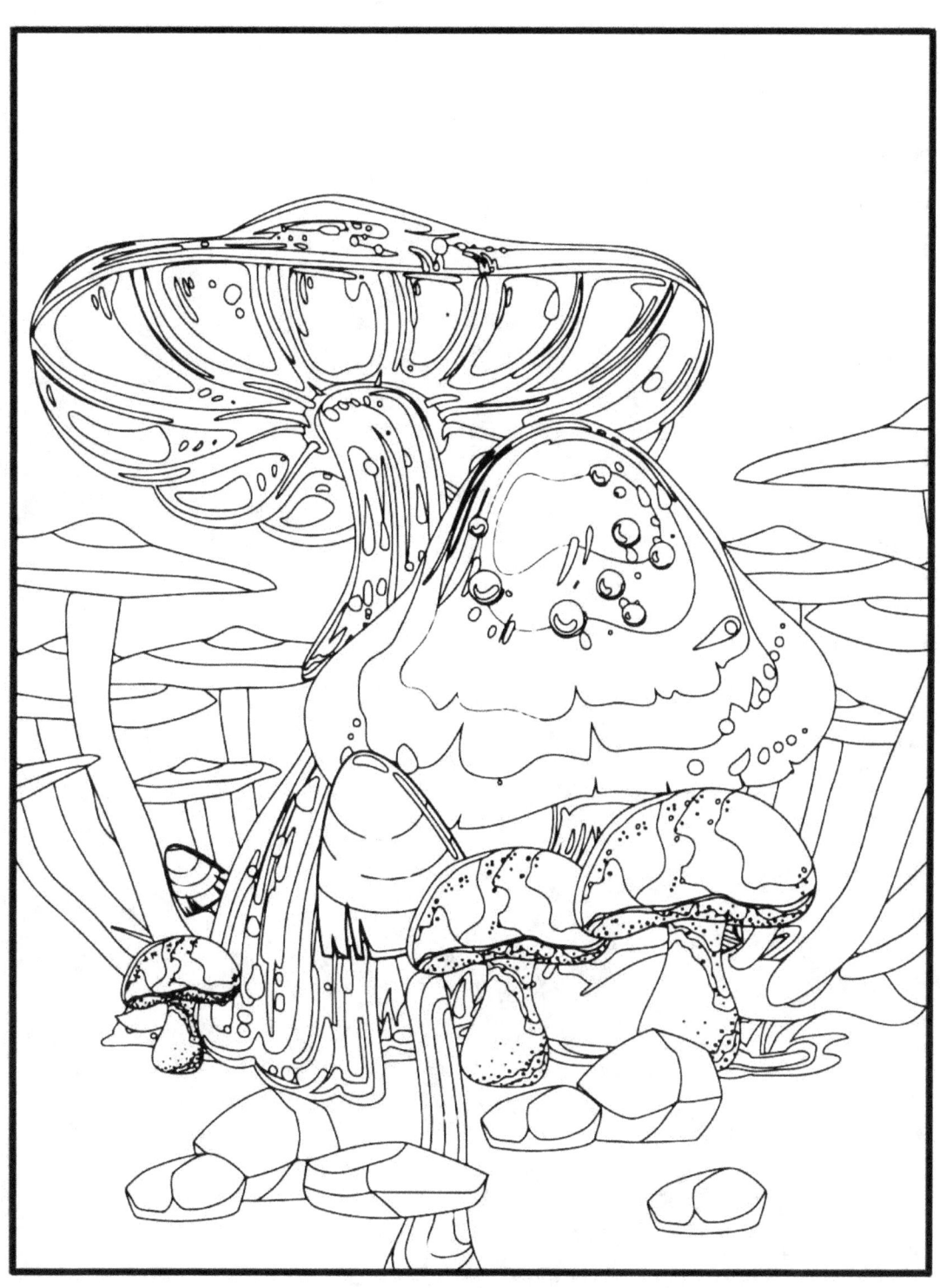

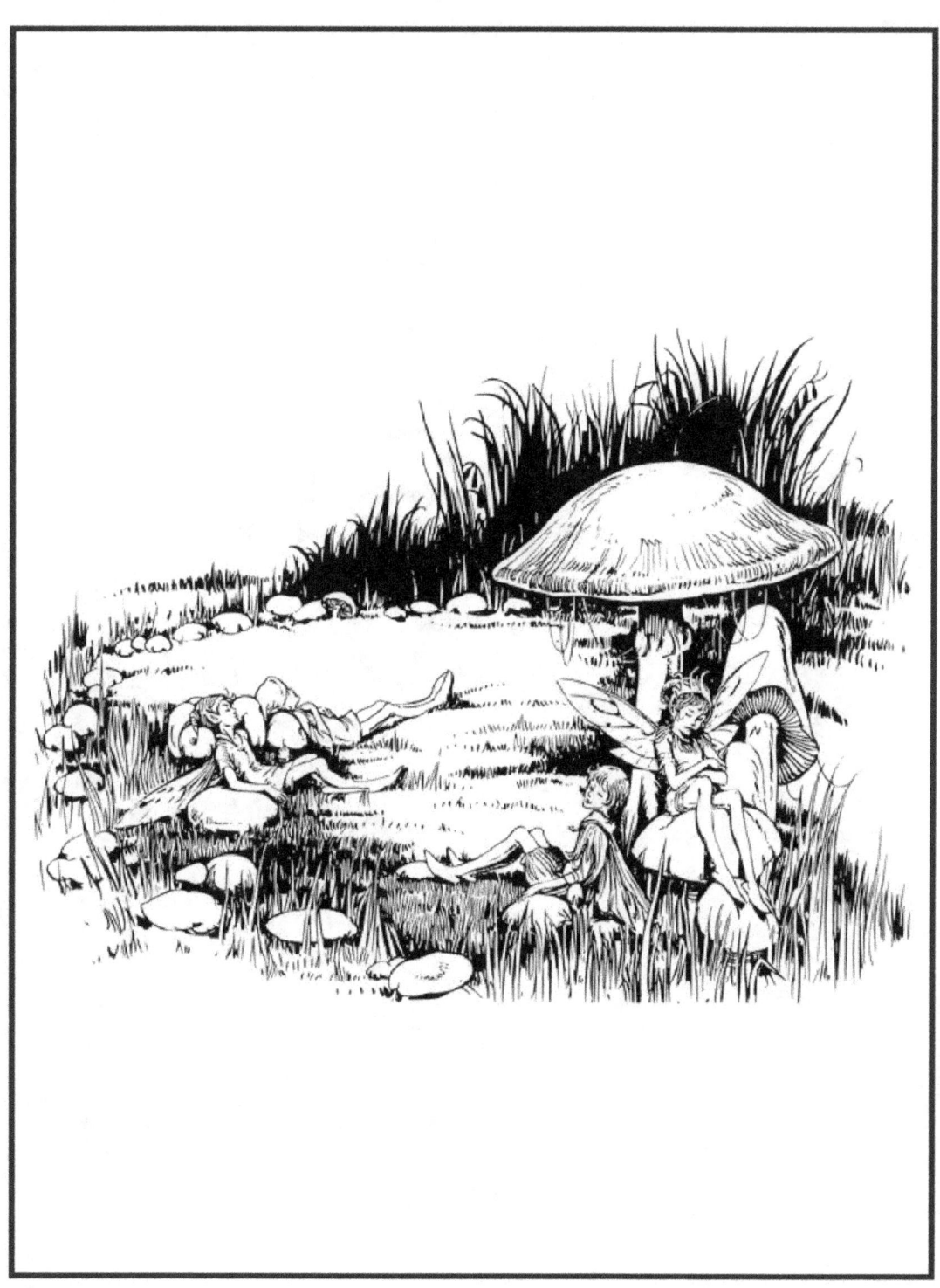

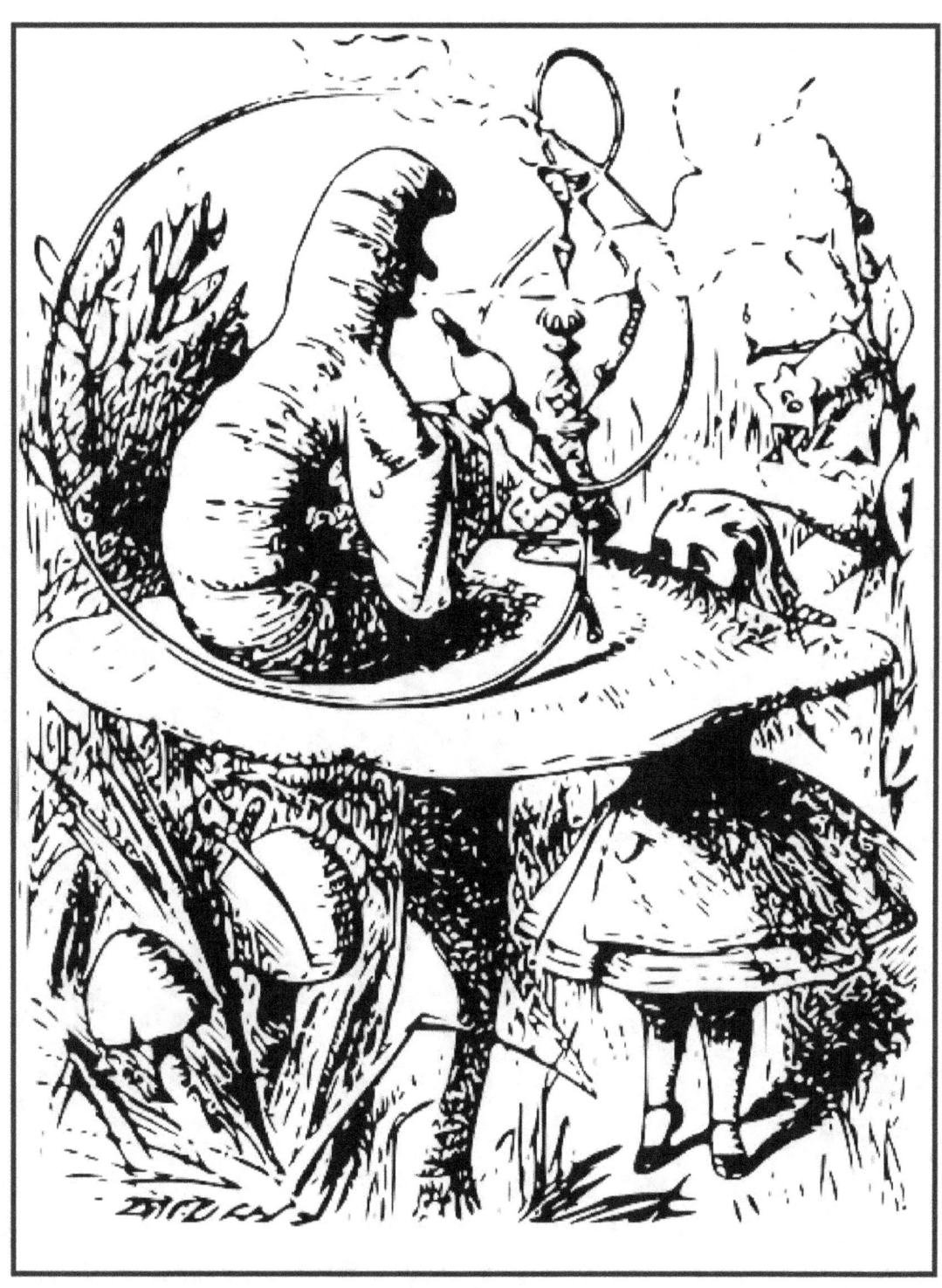